GHOST STORIES
of the
LEHIGH VALLEY

BOOK TWO

by Charles J. Adams III

EXETER HOUSE BOOKS

GHOST STORIES
of the LEHIGH VALLEY
BOOK TWO

© Charles J. Adams III

Published by:
EXETER HOUSE BOOKS
P.O. Box 6411
Wyomissing, PA 19610

www.ExeterHouseBooks.com

PRINTED IN THE UNITED STATES OF AMERICA

TABLE OF CONTENTS

GHOST STORIES OF THE LEHIGH VALLEY (BOOK ONE)
READERS' COMMENTS

I have to admit that I have enjoyed all of the Ghost Stories bookS written by this author. Not only are they an entertaining read, but they have a touch of local culture. I would recommend them to ghost enthusiasts who live in Pennsylvania as well as travelers.

Not only does Adams entertain his reader with a good ghost story, but he usually gives information on the location so the reader can go see for himself. *Ghost Stories of the Lehigh Valley* has some rather nice quality, full page, black and white photos of some of the places mentioned. I even used this book as part of my planning for a haunted Halloween trip with a few friends. With over 20 ghostly tales in just this book, there were plenty from which to choose.

Since moving out of Pennsylvania, I have looked for books on local haunted places in my new home state. I've not found anything as well organized as the series of books by Charles J. Adams III. Each of his books covers one county and only that county. If you're planning a vacation or day trip, it's so nice not to have to dig through an entire state's worth of ghost stories.

Marya, Amazon.com

•

I have lived in the Lehigh Valley area my entire lifetime, and have collected memorabilia and books about the area. But, I cannot recall when I was last intrigued by a book as I have been with
Ghost Stories of the Lehigh Valley.

I was aware of some of these tales, particularly Fred, the ghost at the State Theatre, and the burial ground at Easton Area Public Library. Now, I have those tales, along with all of your other stories of hauntings, ghosts, and the totally unexplained.

I could not put the book down after I began reading it, and the collection of photos of the landmarks you discussed are most valuable in themselves. I sincerely hope that you have derived as much pleasure from your research as I have derived the pleasure
from reading about the places.

Wayne S. Miller

•

**A super, natural companion to this book,
Ghost Stories of the Lehigh Valley (Book One)
is available at booksellers or at**
www.ExeterHouseBooks.com

ABOUT THE AUTHOR
Charles J. Adams III

This is Charlie's 35th book and 23rd specifically dealing with ghosts and haunted places. A native and resident of Reading, Pennsylvania, Charlie (seen with "one foot in the grave" at the St. Andrews Cathedral ruins in Scotland), also writes regular features on travel and local legends in the *Reading Eagle* newspaper. In addition, he is the morning air personality on radio station WEEU in Reading.

Adams has been a speaker at the International Ghost Hunters Alliance and Ghost World conventions in Gettysburg, Pa., and at regional paranormal conferences in New Jersey, Maryland, and Pennsylvania. He has been interviewed on ghostly topics in England, Ireland, South Africa, and on countless American radio and television stations.

He has also appeared on various History Channel shows about haunted places and has served as consultant and on-air "expert" for programs on hauntings and ghosts on The Learning Channel, MTV, and The Travel Channel.

Adams has also organized and escorted tours of haunted places in the United States, England, and Scotland. His travels have afforded him the opportunity to stay in some of the most haunted inns, castles, and hotels in the world.

He has produced, written, and conducted "ghost tours" in Lancaster County, Reading, and Philadelphia, Pa.; Cape May, N.J., and Greenwich Village, New York City. His stories have been selected for inclusion in several anthologies, including "Classic American Ghost Stories" (August House Publishing).

In 2006, he donated nearly 400 books he had collected in his travels to the Exeter Community Library near Reading as the "Charles J. Adams III Paranormal Research Collection." It is recognized as the largest single collection of its kind in any library in the nation.

He has served on the marketing committee of the Reading Symphony Orchestra. He has recited dramatic work with the Reading Symphony Orchestra, Reading Philharmonic Orchestra, and the Reading Pops Orchestra. His play, "Curtains," was produced and presented at the Genesius Theatre, and his "Storybook Murder" mystery was produced and performed as a fund-raising event for the Reading Public Library. He has been co-host of the "YNOTs Awards" show, which recognizes the best of high school musical presentations and performers in Berks County, since its inception.

Charlie has also served as president of the Reading (Pa.) Public Library, was a founding trustee of the Exeter Community Library, and a member of the Board of Directors of the Exeter Township School District. He has also been on the boards of the Penn State Berks Campus Alumni Society, Crestwood Swimming Association, Humane Society of Berks County, and the Historical Society of Berks County. He is presently a member of the editorial board of the Historical Society and is chairman of its Publications Committee.

A singer in rock bands for most of his life, Charlie has written and recorded several folk songs about ghosts, railroads, and baseball. Among his most cherished lifetime achievements were the times he has sung the national anthem, a capella, before a Reading Phillies game.

TITLES PUBLISHED BY EXETER HOUSE BOOKS

Luzerne & Lackawanna Counties Ghosts, Legends and Lore
Haunted Berks County
Tales from Baseballtown
Ghost Stories of Delaware County
Coal Country Ghosts, Legends, and Lore
Atlantic County Ghost Stories
Ghost Stories of Chester County
Montgomery County Ghost Stories
Bucks County Ghost Stories
Philadelphia Ghost Stories
New York City Ghost Stories
Cape May Ghost Stories, Book I
Cape May Ghost Stories, Book II
Cape May Ghost Stories, Book III
Shipwrecks & Legends 'round Cape May
Pocono Ghosts, Legends & Lore, Book I
Pocono Ghosts, Legends & Lore, Book II
Ghost Stories of Pittsburgh & Allegheny Co.
Pennsylvania Dutch Country Ghosts
Ghost Stories of the Lehigh Valley
Ghost Stories of the Lehigh Valley, Book II
Ghost Stories of the Delaware Coast
Shipwrecks, Sea Stories and Legends of the Delaware Coast
Ghost Stories of Berks County, Book I
Ghost Stories of Berks County, Book II
Ghost Stories of Berks County, Book III
Berks the Bizarre
Legends of Long Beach Island
Shipwrecks Near Barnegat Inlet
Shipwrecks Off Ocean City (NJ)
Great Train Wrecks of Eastern Pennsylvania
The New York City Fire Patrol, An Illustrated. History

Books may be ordered at major booksellers or at
www.ExeterHouseBooks.com

INTRODUCTION

What you are about to read has nothing to do with ghost stories or the supernatural. And yet, it has *everything* to do with ghost stories and the supernatural. It strikes at the very heart and soul of both.

Since the early 1980s, I have been prowling the countryside telling ghostly tales to whomever wishes to hear them. With my trusty cape, coachman's hat, an English walking stick, and a vast mental reservoir full of tales to tell, I have ventured hither and yon spinning my yarns to young and old.

Be it on a beach between a dune and the surf of the New Jersey shore, in the gloomy bowels of the walls of old Edinburgh, in a windy, grim castle in Cornwall; or in the auditorium of a school in Pennsylvania, I have endeavored to spark imaginations and nudge audiences to the perilous precipices of their thresholds of fear. Through those decades, my Octobers have been months of days and nights on the road with many miles to go and many stories to tell.

Presenting ghost stories in a book is one thing. The written words flow from my fingers to the computer screen. They are then formatted into pages and books. They are but images of ink and paper.

Telling ghost stories eyeball-to-eyeball; watching those eyeballs widen and roll at the mention of grisly, ghoulish ghosts that may lurk right over the listeners' shoulders; and witnessing a collective shuddering as I speak of things that may go bump in *their* own nights-*that* is when and where stories of the dead come alive not only for them, but for me. I cannot watch those eyes as they read my books. I *can* watch, however, as they listen to my stories.

I like to tell ghost stories. I like to scare people.

I have told ghost stories to gatherings of four and to groups of hundreds, and to folks aged four to one hundred. More likely than not, no matter where I go and to whom I relate the stories, the reactions are generally the same.

They like to hear ghost stories. They like to be scared.

My most recent Halloween ghost storytelling tour came to a stunning and unforgettable end. It had been a long month with 34 ghost tours, book signings, and storytelling programs in 31 days. The "grand finale" was actually the first weekend in November.

The first of those last storytelling events were two sessions in an ancient (and haunted) hotel/restaurant on a Friday night.

In that appropriate venue and in those two seatings of adults, the stories played well. I watched grown men wriggle in their seats at the mention of phantom footsteps coming up a staircase on a quiet night. I smiled inside as otherwise poised women cowered when I told the story of the ghostly wisps of air that caress women as they lay in bed in a suite at a particular local bed and breakfast.

I also explained that to the researcher and writer of ghost stories, Halloween is "amateur night." It is to serious paranormal researchers what New Year's Eve is to a drunk. Ghosts have no calendars, no wristwatches, no PDAs–the energies of which they are comprised are out there 24/7/365.

It was four days past Halloween, but the "holiday" spirit was still very much evident. In each session, filled to the room's capacity, eager ears awaited eerie encounters. I explained that even though Halloween was past for that year, they should consider their event the first of the next year's Halloween season-an early, early start.

I went away from that old hotel feeling that I had done the job I was asked to do. I felt that I had given those folks something to think about, reasons to look over their shoulders every once in a while, stories that just might keep them awake a little bit longer that night.

But, the very last events of the storytelling season would be on the following evening. And, as that evening was approaching, a full moon was rising and Orion was chasing the misty, mysterious nymphs of the constellation Pleiades in their eternal pursuit.

My first engagement on that Saturday night was high atop a hill at a gathering of members of a hiking club.

My charge that night was to tell ghost stories before a bonfire on the edge of a wooded section of the grounds. It was again an adult crowd, and again seemingly anxious to have their senses teased and tormented by my tales.

Before I psyched myself into my "storytelling zone" mood, donned my black hat, grabbed my walking stick, and strolled into their midst, I stood on the lip of hillside that overlooked broad fields and patches of forests draped over a rolling landscape that splayed out north toward the mountains.

The moon, the Harvest Moon no less, was a spotlight that cast the countryside in a silvery glow. Clusters of lights at crossroads or in villages glistened. The only sounds were the breeze

4

whooshing through the woods and the distant crackling of the fire. The only scents were from the pines to my right, the fallen leaves at my feet, and the faint and somehow familiar aroma of the bonfire. I breathed deeply and slowly inhaled this autumnal essence.

I could have stood on that hill, on that night, for hours. But, it was time to tell ghost stories before the fluttering flames and fertile imaginations.

The hour passed all too quickly and I was whisked away to my next appointment in a small town's park. I was anxious to close the storytelling curtain there, as I was to be part of the local historical society's "Harvest Moon Festival." However, the descent into the valley from the literal and figurative loftiness of the previous hilltop venue would probably be anticlimactic.

I couldn't have been more wrong.

As my advance man dropped me off beyond a hedgerow, out of sight from the revelers, I lurked for a few minutes alone in the moon-dusted darkness as the final hayride wagon made its return to the center of the town park. Again, a bonfire was ablaze and again, people gathered around it for warmth and comfort. There, though, it was a more festive mood made so by the presence of many families.

That, of course, can present a challenge to the

teller of terrifying tales. It was, after all, a festival of the harvest, not horror. And, in the skittish society of the 21st century, too many people are hoisting up too many shields against stories that may be too frightening for little imaginations.

But as I have been on the tale trail for three and a half decades, I have learned how far I should and could go with little ones. Certain gory details that are part and parcel to a ghost story are to be told only to older listeners. Indeed, some entire stories are not suitable for more impressionable and innocent ears. I know how to split the differences.

I watched the swarming, warming tangle of youngsters as they toasted marshmallows and roasted hot dogs in the fire. I was enrobed by the aromas of both. I listened to the laughter, and to the picking and singing of traditional Pennsylvania Dutch songs by a local minstrel who engaged all in sing-alongs and silliness.

And then, it was my turn. Having savored all those small-town morsels, I was more in the mood to tell ghost stories than I had ever been, in any other place, ever before. The Harvest Moon beaming from a cloudless sky and the celebration that honored it was pure Americana.

I was to be warmed on the outside by the bonfire before which I would stand for the next hour. I had already been warmed thoroughly on the inside by the sights, sounds, and smells of all that is good about fall in Pennsylvania.

But, I had ghost stories to tell before I could sample a brownie and sip some cider. So, to center stage I sauntered and stood in the fiery spotlight. My cloaked countenance and my silent prowling elicited a hush as families bundled up and cuddled together.

Chilly children were chilled further by the stories. They cringed at the saga of the headless ghost that stumbles through a nearby covered bridge, searching for its head that was severed in an ancient accident. They gasped at the ghoulish goings-on in a graveyard in their own hometown. They recoiled when I suggested there might be phantoms haunting their very bedrooms-later that night.

From the opening "It was a dark and stormy night..." to the closing "Sleep tight tonight," I had 'em. More correctly, the ghost stories, the full moon, and the bonfire had 'em.

And if there were any real ghosts hovering there that night, it would have been the spirit of Norman Rockwell, peering down with a smile on its face.

Thank you for reading this book,
Charles J. Adams III

THE CELLAR DWELLER

Christopher Bohar freely admits he has a deep interest in the realm of the paranormal.

He also admits that he has been aware of residents of that realm since he was a young boy.

His stories played out in an unremarkable ca. 1929 home in Freemansburg. "I have lived in this house all my life," he said, "and have always had a pretty firm belief in the idea of life after death."

He said his first encounter with the unknown was in 1989, when he was only about five years old.

"My parents were renovating the house, tearing apart the first and second floors and I was forced along with my brother to share the basement until we could move back into our rooms. The basement was basically one gigantic space with the stairs running down the middle. I recall one night I was awakened by what appeared to what I can best describe as a 'three dimensional shadow' that was standing about three feet in front of the bed.

"I woke my brother who was about 14 at the time and he saw the same thing I did. This entity was holding what looked like a staff in his right hand, and he was quite slender and very tall–at least six and a half feet tall if not more. I recall we were so frightened we began looking at the wall opposite us in the hopes he would go away but this entity began to slowly pace in front of the bed as if he was curious. We could make out no facial features. Now, there is a small sort of hallway where the water heater is on the left hand side of the basement that you can access through a small doorway a few feet front of the foot of where the bed once was.

"About ten minutes after we first sighted this tall spirit entity it simply walked through this doorway and we never saw him again. I theorize all the activity of renovation probably stirred him up."

Chris's experiences in the house were not limited to the basement.

"The next startling encounter I had was in the upstairs of the house, where my bedroom is located. To start off we had an Irish deerhound named Mutley, a very loyal animal who we unfortunately had to put to sleep after 14 years with us due to arthritis and old age.

"This was around April, 2001. About a month after that happened, during both the day and nighttime hours I began to hear a sound very familiar to myself during Mutley's life. She had the habit of lying on the top landing and wagging her tail up against the wooden doors. I was watching television upstairs one day and I heard that sound against the closed door as clear as could be.

"Surprisingly, it did not frighten me in the least, but I got the definite sensation that the dog's spirit had returned and had taken her usual perch up on the top landing. I also began to hear her licking her paws when this occurred–which was another one of her habits in life as well. This was not an isolated incident either and this went on almost daily for an hour or more at a time for at least a year if not longer.

"It was not until my dad brought home a new black lab we named Onyx that this phenomenon ceased–although my father has claimed he saw Mutley in the back yard by the tool shed one afternoon while doing yard work.

"Another strange phenomenon that has happened to me is hearing my name called. I would come home from work after the second shift and lay down on the couch to relax and often here a very soft voice whisper 'Chris'–even while I was wide awake. This has happened when I have been alone in the house and has been quite unsettling as it still occurs from time to time.

"At first, I tried to rationalize it away as a byproduct of being tired. But to hear it so clearly and frequently even while being quite lucid made me wonder who it could possibly be. Maybe it's a former occupant of the house, as the voice does not sound as if it belongs to any deceased relatives that I know of."

Chris said the incidents of his childhood and adolescence spurred him to take an interest in the paranormal as a young adult. Alas, those episodes are tucked deeply in his memory.

"Nowadays," he continued, "the spirits seemed to have either quieted down or found peace on another plane where they belong. The incident of the tall figure in the basement was the only time I really ever felt threatened by the activity, but I attribute that to being so young at the time.

"Being a amateur paranormal investigator myself, I have investigated other peoples' homes and have heard of similar phenomena involving animals and 'shadow people,' but most paranormal investigators cannot truly appreciate eyewitness testimony until it occurs to them personally."

At times, telling others about his experiences has been awkward. Sometimes they write him and his stories off. Sometimes, though, they become hesitant believers.

"An ex-girlfriend of mine was at my house one time," he said, "and she had a change of heart when she entered the kitchen and a cabinet door opened by itself! Several of my other friends told me they have gotten strange vibes from my home, especially on the first floor.

"Again, though, I have never felt unwelcome by the entities but I feel many ghosts are as curious and perhaps frightened of us as we are of them."

•

THE ROADSIDE GHOST

There are times when I feel I am trading credibility for anonymity when I relate the tales of individuals who prefer that their names or addresses or both not be published.

I am sensitive to their requests, of course. Often, the person telling the story wishes to remain nameless because of their position or status in the community. Or, they may want to shield family members, friends, or neighbors from any and all repercussions from situations that are far outside the comfort zones of many people.

I can only ask the reader to share that sensitivity and, at the same time, trust that although names and places are changed or omitted, the stories are true as told by the tellers.

In this story, the names are indeed changed, and the exact location of the haunting will not be revealed.

"If you pinpointed the spot in your book," the man we shall call Pete said, "I'm afraid too many curious people might congregate there and ruin things."

We can say that Pete is a 29-year old man who lives near Slatington, and he is convinced that the ghost of an old friend remains earthbound.

And, his story is unlike any other we have ever heard in more than 35 years of collecting and dispensing ghost stories and investigating hauntings.

Pete was visibly emotional as he started to speak.

"This will be hard to tell in an 'official' way," he said, pausing to take a deep breath. "I have only shared it with friends I trusted would not think I went off the deep end. Even when I think about what happened, and continues to happen, I even question my own sanity!"

Pete is quite sane, quite rational. In fact, one of the reasons he did not want his real name used is that he is in a position of respect and trust with a great number of people. "If some of them knew it was me telling the story," he said, "I'm afraid they would lose some of that trust we have built up over the years."

After another deep breath, he went into detail about the incidents that introduced him to the realm of the unexplainable.

"I'll start at the beginning," he continued. "My good friend Gary was a fun-loving guy who loved to go rafting up the river, take long–very long–bicycle rides, and enjoyed just about any outdoor activity. He was a good skier–I was better–and was starting to get into bird identification and viewing. I'd like to think that he was my best friend.

"He dated several girls, but said he would never get married until, as he used to say, 'all the planets aligned' and the absolute, positive, 'right one' came along.

"Everybody liked Gary. He was always good for a laugh. He was just a good guy.

"Well, one morning last fall, I got one of those phone calls you never expect to get, and never want to get. It was another friend who had been informed that Gary had been in a very serious car crash and was fighting for his life in the hospital.

"Damn, I thought, this can't be. Not Gary, no! I asked if there was anything I could do, or if I could see Gary in the hospital. Then, my friend, who was very close to Gary's family and a trained EMT, broke down and told me the truth. Gary was actually killed instantly when his car slammed into a tree. It was a pretty violent crash, I was later told."

Again, Pete said he preferred that the exact location of the accident not be published–for reasons that will soon become obvious.

"Well," he continued, "I found out that Gary just lost control of his car and ran off the road. He wasn't exactly a daredevil driver. In fact, because he was a volunteer firefighter and saw his share of grisly accidents, he always buckled up and didn't take chances.

"He was alone when he had the accident, so we'll never know the real reason he lost control. I would like to believe that one of the cops who was first on the scene was right when he said it might have been a case of the driver, Gary, swerving to avoid hitting a deer or other animal, and veering into the tree."

Pete's eyes welled with tears as he related several vignettes about his deceased friend and the good times they had over the years.

"He was missed by many people," Pete said. "We were in shock for several days, through the funeral and all.

"It wasn't until we got together after Gary was buried that I learned exactly where the accident took place. I knew that stretch of road well, but hadn't been up that way for a long time. But, I could more or less picture where Gary crashed."

While he did say on what road and where the accident happened, we shall refer to it simply as a road somewhere in northwestern Lehigh County.

At Gary's wake, Pete was urged to go along with one of Gary's brothers and another friend and mark the site of the crash with a small memorial. They figured they would place some flowers from the funeral around some sort of symbolic thing from Gary's life. What they settled on was a ski boot filled with stones to anchor it. It really wasn't planned to be permanent, just something that soothed the minds of those who knew him best. Personally, I'm against those roadside shrine things, but I didn't express my thoughts to those who were gung-ho to put it up.

"Actually, I thought those things were kind of morbid, but I guess I understood why they did it."

Pete grieved for his friend in his own way, and went about his life.

"I guess it was about a month after Gary died when I was headed to Tamaqua. As I made my way over the back, I thought it might be good to swing a mile or so off the route and pay a visit to the crash site. I guess they call it closure."

In an absolutely incredible turn of events, however, Pete's visit to the spot Gary died provided anything but closure.

Pete took yet another deep breath, threw his head back, and closed his eyes. "Here's where it gets weird," he sighed. "Here's where it gets *really* weird."

Pete reiterated that he was not fabricating the story and was still reluctant to see it in a book, even if the names were changed.

"I turned onto the road where Gary had his accident and went around a couple of curves until

I got onto the short straight-away where it happened, and that's where everything went absolutely crazy.

"I approached the spot where the crash happened. Just up the road, maybe 100 feet, I saw the road sign they told me Gary hit before he smashed his car into the tree. The sign had been remounted, and even from that distance I could see the scars and stripped bark on the big tree. I got chills.

"But, that was nothing. I slowed down and saw a little bunch of something colorful just off the side of the road. I knew it was the memorial to Gary. I got the chills again.

"And, you can believe this or not, but as I got closer I witnessed something that nearly made *me* lose control of my car and drive off the road.

"I was maybe 50 feet from the memorial, going very slow, when out of the stand of trees that surrounded the tree Gary crashed into came what looked like a stiff wind. Otherwise, it was not at all windy, as I can recall. But, I watched in amazement as the trees shook, leaves flew, and that one blast of wind came through.

"And then...and I have a hard time saying this...from those trees came Gary. I had not given ghosts or anything like that much thought in my life, but I will swear in court or church that out of the woods, and out of that wind came the very clear vision of my dead friend Gary!"

Pete had been nursing a cup of coffee as we talked, but at the mention of the "vision" of his friend emerging from the woods, his hands trembled too much for him to grip the coffee cup. Through quivering lips, he continued his story.

"I slowed down to a crawl, and without any doubt in my mind whatsoever I saw Gary standing just behind the little roadside memorial, near the tree he hit.

"It seemed as if he was totally oblivious to the fact that I, or anyone, was near. I can't say if he was walking, or gliding, or floating. I can't say I could make out any facial emotions. But it was most certainly Gary.

"I hit the brakes when the vision first appeared. I was startled, as you might imagine. But, I kept going slow past the memorial, the tree, and then the vision of Gary. I was both confused, amazed, and a little bit scared.

"Never did I think it was some sort of a joke or prank. It wasn't someone trying to look like him, it was Gary.

"The form–the ghost, I guess you can call it–just seemed to stay at one place for maybe ten seconds as I drove by. I had to take my eyes off him for a split second to watch the road ahead, and when I looked back, the vision was gone."

A sense of tranquility swept over Pete as he

finished his story.

"You're the first stranger I ever told this to," he added. "In fact, I have only told one other person about it. She was one of Gary's closest friends, and she wrote off my experience as just my vivid imagination. Just to appease her, I nodded, smiled, and agreed with her. But, what I saw that day was not imaginary."

Pete said he has baited other friends of Gary to try to see if any of them have driven past the memorial and had the same experience. There is no indication any have–or have chosen to admit it.

"If it wasn't my imagination," Pete asked, "and I know it wasn't...then, what was it? I kept asking myself that."

So, how did Pete answer himself?

"I would like to believe that what I saw was Gary's spirit appearing at the very spot he died to somehow, as I have heard it said, 'give me a sign' to let me know he's still around. Since then, I've done some research on all of that, and I have also come to realize that Gary's spirit may also have been there because it hadn't crossed to the 'other side' or gone into the light. I can only hope that if that's the case, he finds peace wherever it may be found.

"Someday, I might head up that way and see what I can see. Until then, I'm still too creeped out from that last encounter."

I asked Pete if he would accompany me to the spot of Gary's death. He begged off, saying that as unnerving as the last encounter might have been, he prefers to keep that experience, and that vision of his old friend, locked in his mind.

I decided I had to satiate my own curiosity by venturing to the the crash site.

Following directions Pete provided, I found the lonely road upon which Gary lived the last frantic moments of his life.

The fireman's boot is gone from the shrine, replaced by a crude cross and a handful of fading, fake flowers. The fallen leaves of autumn all but covered the remains of the memorial.

The tree still bears scars from the crash, but even they are healing.

Alone there, I lingered. I mentally and psychically called for Gary (invoking his actual name) to give me a sign.

I repeated the urging several times.

Nothing. Not a breeze through the trees, not a vision, not even an eerie feeling. I recalled some of Pete's stories about Gary, smiled, and bid farewell to the young man I never met, but came to know through his friend's memories.

I would like to think that Gary really did make that final appearance for Pete and found his way to that peaceful place.

But then again.....

MAGGIE

The Center Valley Tavern is a survivor. Situated on the northbound lanes of Route 309 (officially, 6034 Main Street) in the village of Center Valley, the tavern has served several functions and several masters over the years.

Its present master, er, mistress, is Jane Logan, who conceded that a ghost may well walk the stairs and floors of the building.

Jane was a bit reluctant to discuss any hauntings

in the building because she not only works there by day, but sleeps there by night. As it turned out, both her workplace and living spaces are visited by the two ghosts that dwell inside.

She was only told about one of the spirits there, but has had a firsthand encounter with the other.

Jane recounted the story of a former owner of the inn who died in the tiny men's room to the rear of the bar several decades ago.

"People have told me that when they have come in here, they have seen a male figure standing behind the bar, near the men's room door," she said.

She learned of the men's room ghost when she purchased the tavern. She was told that the old proprietor's body was found in the men's room, and many patrons not only believed his ghost remained in the rear area of the bar, but several have seen a filmy and flimsy apparition in the area.

While she has never seen that male spirit, she *has* seen at least one other ghost that haunts the place.

"At the top of the stairs," she said, matter-of-factly, "is a colonial lady."

She described the woman as a woman in late 18th-century dress, silently maintaining a vigil at one spot at the top of a staircase that leads to the living area of the building.

"One of my psychic, sensitive friends came upstairs and she said the ghost was a young woman who was waiting there for her boyfriend," she said.

That would be a boyfriend who never returned. "She said the woman's boyfriend was shot an killed in a duel or some sort of gunplay, to the rear of the building," Jane added.

In addition to the psychic's vision of the Center Valley Tavern's resident *female* ghost, Jane said her energy actually showed up as an anomaly on the field of vision of a surveillance camera.

"She–it–doesn't frighten me," she continued. "I'd just like to know more about her. I'd like to know who she was, and more of the story about how her boyfriend was killed. I just wonder who the heck she might be!"

Jane has arbitrarily given her the name "Maggie." And, Maggie just might have helped the tavern continue to survive.

"One time," Jane said, "we were drying towels in a dryer downstairs. No big deal. But then, I got this feeling that Maggie was telling me to go downstairs immediately.

"At first, I shrugged it off. But then, a few minutes later, I smelled something burning. I got downstairs, and a small fire had broken out. I managed to douse it, but who knows, without Maggie, what might have happened?!"

THE ETERNAL ENCORE

Brad Youst, the technical director of the Pennsylvania Playhouse, had indicated that there had been some, shall we say, *disturbances* in the popular theater that could be attributed to spectral activity.

Brad grew up a couple miles from the Bethlehem showplace and has been a volunteer there since 1974. He is as familiar with the inner workings of the theater as anyone else, and he was kind enough to take us into the many rooms behind the stage.

To get there, of course, we had to proceed from the lobby, where we met, and through the auditorium of what he called the "theater-in-the-corner" (as opposed to "in-the-round"–we'll explain later).

As Brad opened the doors to the "house," he fully expected to encounter a ghost.

A ghost *light*, that is.

But, to our surprise and his chagrin, the ghost light of the playhouse had not been lit. And, that could well have been interpreted as a sign.

Visibly perturbed, Brad commented, "It's distressing, because we have it there as total tradition and total respect for whomever occupies this place when we're not here."

For the uninitiated, a ghost light is a fascinating theater tradition with deep roots in both the practical and the paranormal.

When the marquee lights are ablaze, crooking their fingers of beckoning illumination, a theater is an inviting place.

When patrons shuffle down aisles and into their seats, the house lights bathe their anticipation with the reassuring glow that the show is about to go on.

And, when those lights dim and the curtain opens, the stage lights cast their brilliance on those who will transport the audience into a land of make-believe.

But when the last curtain call–the final encore–has been taken...when the lights are left to cool...when the last of the audience has left...a theater becomes a dark, almost foreboding kind of place.

By its very nature, a theater is a vault within which every human emotion is at once imprisoned, impersonated, imitated, and elicited. Tangles of ropes and cords...tall curtains and backdrops that fade into high darkness...cubicles and trap doors and passageways....the classic theater is itself a fantasy world with its own tales to tell and its own cast of characters who have come, gone, and perhaps remain.

One of the most bizarre, baffling, awe-inspiring, and thought-provoking icons of the mysteries of the theatrical community is the "Ghost Light."

What is a ghost light? Why a ghost light?

The notion of ghosts is an ancient tradition in the theatrical world.

There was once a phrase in the theater... *"When the ghost walks..."*

As mysterious as it may sound, it is just an ancient reference to payday in the theater office.

That "ghost" that "walked" on payday was none other than an actor who played Hamlet in a Shakespearian company long, long ago. He was also the paymaster! That dual role vaulted him into theater lore for many generations of actors who eagerly awaited the walk of the money-toting ghost.

But what of the ghost light?

When the curtain closes, the last player and patron leaves the auditorium, and when all the house lights are switched off, this simple bulb–and long ago it would have been a lantern–is switched on. It remains lighted throughout the night until the cast and crew return.

It is said that this single lamp serves to soothe the spirits that may wander through the theater. As the story goes, if a theater is ever left completely dark, the ghosts within it will rise and ramble.

So, when Brad Youst opened the auditorium doors and found that the house was totally dark, it was a bit unsettling and, perhaps, ominous.

"I'd like to think that the ghost light is here so that when we're not, they have lighting to do their plays," he said–not entirely kiddingly.

Some theaters have even named their ghost lights. The Pennsylvania Playhouse has not given a sobriquet to its ghost light, but in tributes to a former lighting men, their work lights are nicknamed "Humphreys" and the light board is called "Fred."

That is germane to the story as it is a tribute to the theatrical traditions–and superstitions–that many at the playhouse hold dearly to their artistic hearts.

"We're not an ancient house here," Brad continued. "The theater was built in 1965. But, we have had a lot of people here, and many have crossed to the other side, Stefan for one."

Stefan is, to those who believe, the most likely to be the star of the ghostly show at the Pennsylvania Playhouse.

"Oh yes," Brad said, "we all think that Stefan has made this place his home *after* his home."

He is speaking of Stefan George, whom with his wife Rita were backbones of many plays and players at the playhouse. He was a fixture there for many years, and truly did call it home at times. "He actually did live here at times, staying overnight," Brad added.

"Stefan was a taskmaster of characterization. He really felt that the play was the thing. He didn't really care much for the setting. He wanted the actors to pull it off.

"He just felt the theater–this theater–was his home, and he wanted to come back. We think he did, and continues to!"

That translates to the theory that the eternal energies of Stefan George might still be contained inside the walls of the playhouse.

"We have had many people work at the theater," Brad said, "and many people who have spent the kinds of hours that I do, doing tech work after rehearsals, etc., who can get to experience the theater at the time of day when everybody else is out. It's quiet, and you have the whole place to itself. So, you have the atmosphere, the essence, the smells, the sounds of the theater, and they are all around you.

"More than once, people working that shift around here, into the deep hours of the night, have experienced things that can't really be well explained.

"Once, on a quiet night, while setting light cues, the sound of water running backstage could clearly be heard. That has been heard since, frequently.

"We'd get up from the auditorium seats, walk downstairs, and there would be water running in the sink in the dressing room. The doors were locked, lights were off, nobody around, but the water was running in the sink. And, everybody knew the water wasn't left running from rehearsal."

Another indication that ethereal energies may be putting on a show in the theater is the occasional rattling of doors that separate the dressing room and a back prop storage and work room.

"At times, the wind might rattle them," Brad speculated. "But, there are also times that we hear them slamming a lot more than the wind could ever do."

"Some people said that they have heard voices in the theater when and where there was nobody anywhere nearby."

Brad Youst, technical director at the Pennsylvania Playhouse, said these doors have been known to "rattle" on their own, possibly indicating the presence of ghost in the house.

Another person intimate with the ins and outs of the Pennsylvania Playhouse is Helen Manderbach, who has been an actor, director, and

31

supporter of the playhouse since its days "under the bridge" in Bethlehem. She was there when it was the Bethlehem Civic Theater, she was there when it moved to its present location on Illicks Mill Road, and she was there when a fire gutted the theater on New Year's Eve, 1974. It was after that tragedy when the theater was rebuilt with a square "thrust" stage in one corner of the rectangular auditorium (hence, the "theater-in-the-corner" moniker). That "essence" of that theater is in her blood.

As Helen fondly recalled her many years at the playhouse, she could not dismiss the possibility that those who have poured so much emotion and love into the shows and production have left some of their energies there. And, she agreed that Stefan might be the most likely denizen of the darkened house.

"He was a real artist," she remembered. "He sometimes stayed overnight. It could be Stefan. But, if anybody really made a 'home' at the playhouse, it would have been Hunt Mathews. He was everywhere."

And, who knows? He may still be there.

Stewart Hunt Mathews, a.k.a. "Hunt," was described as a rather eccentric chap who was also dedicated to the playhouse and spent many days and nights there.

"We called him 'Mr. Instant Forest,'" said

Brad Youst. "He could take a piece of canvas and paint an absolutely gorgeous outdoor setting on any surface for any needs we had.

"Yes, Hunt is quite possibly here, too. He spent so much time here in the early days of the theater, and it was a home away from home for him, so his spirit may also be here."

Helen Manderbach did have a brush with another theater ghost in the Lehigh Valley several years ago.

"We moved our cast of '1776' to Easton when they were trying to revive the State Theatre and we were one of the productions they brought in. I was there, the cast had left, and the musical director asked if I would go backstage with him. He said he didn't like going there by himself. He told me, 'this place is full of ghosts!' Well, I laughed. Then, though, he told me about the time the police were actually called because someone heard footsteps running in the theater."

[Note: The story of "Freddie," the ghost of the State Theatre, was detailed in our first *Ghost Stories of the Lehigh Valley* book].

Whether his ghost dwells at the playhouse is debatable, but there is absolutely no doubt whatsoever that Stefan George, and his wife Rita really do remain forever at the Pennsylvania Playhouse. Before they passed, the requested that their ashes be buried in the garden at the entrance to the theater.

There, indeed, they rest...in peace.

WELCOME, MR. FINK!

Joshua Arthur Fink became a tour director of the Liberty Bell Shrine Museum in Allentown in the late 1990s. He has since advanced to the position of curator of the museum that recalls the city's unique contribution to the fight for freedom in the 18th century.

A chapter in any textbook of American history will tell the tale of Gen. George Washington's army spending the winter of 1777-78 at Valley Forge.

A footnote to that chapter would be where and why an American icon spent that same winter.

It was the worst of times for the colonists'

cause. The British had soundly defeated the Americans at the Battle of Brandywine in the early autumn of 1777 and went on to occupy the colonial capital of Philadelphia.

Washington's troops regrouped at Valley Forge. The Continental Congress fled to Lancaster and then York. Munitions and supplies were stashed in Reading.

The Continental Congress feared the British might melt down the bells of Philadelphia's churches and Pennsylvania State House and remanufacture them into bullets. So, it came up with a plan to pack 11 of the most important bells onto wagons, disguise them under a covering of manure and hay, and haul them some 60 miles north to Northampton Towne for safekeeping.

That safety was found under the floorboards of Zion's Reformed Church in that small town along the Lehigh River. For nine of the most critical months of the American Revolution, the bells–including that State House bell–were safe and sound until the Redcoats evacuated Philadelphia in June, 1778 and the bells were taken back to their belfries.

Northampton Towne is now Allentown. Zion's Reformed is now Zion's Reformed United Church of Christ. The State House bell is now known as the Liberty Bell.

The Liberty Bell is, of course, an attraction in

the heart of historic Philadelphia. But, its hiding place during those nine months of 1777-78 was also preserved as the Liberty Bell Shrine.

The Liberty Bell Shrine is now the Liberty Bell Museum, so re-designated as it has broadened its mission since it opened during the church and city's bicentennial years in 1962.

As Joshua Fink advanced within his roles, the museum has also grown since he became its curator in 2003.

It may not be much of a stretch to believe that he has achieved those personal and professional successes with some guidance from the "other side."

"Soon after I started there," he said, "I was standing at the top of the steps doing some work in our gift shop area.

"I looked down and I saw a man standing there. He was a short, little man with a bald head. He was holding the 'clapper catcher' that holds the clapper to the side of the bell to ring it.

"I thought, what the heck–how did this man get in there?"

Joshua had a full view of the museum and surely would have noticed someone ambling by. But, the man he saw by the "star" of the museum seemed to emerge as if out of nowhere. "He was just standing there reverently," Josh added, "as if he was waiting for someone to come down the steps."

He continued, "Then, I turned away for a second and he was gone!"

Josh said who, or what, he saw appeared to be an actual person, but he noticed no motion or emotion. And, as mysteriously as he appeared, he vanished.

"It was all very quick," he said.

A bit confused and confounded by the matter, Josh descended the steps into the main room of the museum for a look around. He saw nothing, no one.

He did know and note that the former curator had died not long before Josh got the job at the museum.

"I saw a photograph of him later," Josh said, "and the figure I saw that day looked very much like the deceased director of the shrine."

"THE DEVIL ONE NIGHT SLEW, DISMEMBERED, AND CARRIED AWAY FROM THE CEMETERY..."

Jerusalem Western Salisbury Graveyard

THE LEGEND OF TAMBOUR YOKEL

It is always uncomfortable and sometimes impossible to secure "official" and attributable information about hauntings in churches. While the basic tenets of religion and the notion of an "afterlife" *(vis-à-vis, ghost)* seem compatible, some less enlightened people reject the paranormal.

Interestingly, however, is that tales of non-Holy ghosts have long been used as morality lessons (and, just plain scary stories) for congregations and have taken their place in local folklore.

Such is the case with a folk ballad recorded and related by Dr. Joseph Henry Dubbs in the late 19th century. It appeared in *Home Ballads and Metrical Versions,* a collection of poems and verses gathered from around eastern Pennsylvania.

In the preface to his book, Dubbs noted, "In composing the historical pieces the writer was conscious of a desire to honor the memory of several of our almost forgotten pioneers, and at the same time to indicate a way by which our rich stores of legend and folk-lore might be employed for literary purposes."

Dr. Dubbs was a Lancaster County historian, theologian, and author who published several volumes about the history of the Reformed Church.

While Dr. Dubbs never pinpointed the church and graveyard settings of the following legend, in his 1976 booklet about the history of Salisbury Township, William L.F. Schmehl placed it at the Western Salisbury Church.

Writer and educator Kelly Ann Butterbaugh had learned about the legend several years ago and shared the township history article with this writer.

In it, Schmehl wrote: "The congregation grew slowly, probably from the formation of others nearby. At the close of the 18th century, when the log structure became dilapidated and unsafe, the church was abandoned; the group was too small and poor to erect another building."

And, Schmehl's next paragraph vaulted the story into the pages of books such as this: "Another reason for its abandonment was the gruesome story of how, soon after the Revolutionary War, the devil one night slew, dismembered, and carried away from the cemetery the body of Tambour Yokel. The story shook up the community so much that people would drive several miles out of the way to avoid passing the cemetery."

Here, following Dr. Dubbs' introduction, is that "gruesome story:"

THE LEGEND OF TAMBOUR YOKEL

The following legend is related–sometimes with fanciful exaggerations–concerning an ancient churchyard in Lehigh county, Pennsylvania. The story can be traced for more than a century. Whatever may have been its historic foundation, it is certain that, a few years ago, it was very generally credited. It was always told with due solemnity, as an example of the mysterious punishment of a dreadful crime.

Tell the story with bated breath–
A story of horror, and gloom, and death.
A little church on a lonely hill;
A churchyard near it, calm and still;
Pair in the morning's early light;
Dark and gloomy it seems at night.
There it is said, in the olden time,
Happened a nameless deed of crime;
And stalwart men, with swiftest pace,
Haste when they pass that dreadful place.
Home, with the troop, from the war had come
Tambour Yokel, who beat the drum:
A worthless wretch, who on his way
Had learned but the arts of a bird of prey;
Who had sold, it was said, in the dreadful strife,
His soul to Satan to save his life.
"Now where," he cried, "is my ancient foe?
I have come from the battle to lay him low."
"Peace! Peace!" they answered. "Your boast is vain;
The man will never fight again;
The foe you hated, and sought to kill,
Now rests in the churchyard on the hill,"
"Ho ! What of that?" the drummer cried,
Perhaps it was well the coward died;
But I know a way, as you'll see to-night,
To bring the man from his grave to fight.
Then a dreadful oath the ruffian swore,
He would call him forth to fight once more.
In their cups that night, at the tavern near,
His comrades met him with mock and jeer:
"Ho, wizard!" they cried. "Why don't you go
To the churchyard now to meet your foe?"
Then Tambour Yokel cursed and swore,
And sallied forth from the tavern door."
Come forth!" he cried, through the startled night, "Come forth, thou
fiend, from the grave and fight!"
He reached the churchyard gate, and then
The fearful challenge was heard again.
But soon a cry that was wild and shrill
Was heard from the churchyard on the hill.
"Help! help! " he cried, but none drew near,
His comrades trembled, aghast with fear,

41

In silence waiting–that godless crew–
While the cries still fainter and fainter grew.
Next morning they came, with silent tread,
Seeking their comrade among the dead.
There, 'mid the graves, the man they found,
Naked and cold on the trodden ground;
Scattered his garments, far and wide;
Bloody the soil where the wretch had died.
And this was all; but who can tell
Who wounded the victim, and how he fell ?
Did a panther, perchance, of the forest tear
The limbs of the wretched boaster there?
Or, was it the fiend, as the neighbors say,
That bore his godless soul away?
Ah! none could tell–nor cared to know–
But a mighty hand had laid him low.
Yet, with a shudder, men still relate
The tale of Tambour Yokel's fate;
And none forgets the legend grim-
How a fearful judgment was sent to him.

(Source: *Home Ballads and Metrical Versions* by Joseph Henry Dubbs, D.D. (Published by Charles G. Fisher, Philadelphia, 1888)

Does the specter of the "wretched boaster" still prowl the graveyard of what is now Jerusalem Western Salisbury Union Church? Have people forgotten the "legend grim?" Do folks still drive several miles around the cemetery to avoid encountering the grisly ghost?

The answer to that last question would have to be "not likely." The Allentown suburbs have extended to what was once an isolated, eerie setting.

The ancient cemetery clings to the side of the church as the sanctuary itself clings to a promontory over the rugged ravine of the Little Lehigh Creek. Even with schools, homes, and commercial development closing in on it, the tree-shaded grove of graves is a serene place. Flags flutter above the final resting places of several veterans; a soft, green moss shrouds some of the markers that range from sturdy, 200 year-old headstones carved in High German to forlorn stone stumps.

Rising above all of them is a memorial to the "several" Indians of the Delaware tribe who are buried on the grounds.

The tranquility of the cemetery befits the historic landmark church, which was founded in 1741. But, it belies the gruesome fate of poor Tambour Yokel oh, so long ago.

But, does his ghost linger forever among the weathered tombstones? Is there really still cause for concern and reason to make a wide berth around the burial ground for fear of encountering Tambour's spirit or drawing the wrath of "the fiend" who tore him to shreds?

I'll meet you there at the stroke of midnight on the next full moon. You bring the lantern!

THE CONDUCTOR

For several years I have led ghost tours for employees of the Lehigh Valley Hospital network, guiding them to and through haunted sites across eastern Pennsylvania.

As I let it be known that I was seeking information about haunted places for a second *Ghost Stories of the Lehigh Valley* book, the buzz on the bus centered around the story of "the conductor" at the former Allentown General Hospital at 17th and Chew Streets.

Several folks who had worked at the hospital

were rather nonchalant about the tale, as if to say "everybody knows that story."

I knew nothing about it, but eagerly sought to find out more.

The organizer of the tours, Nancy Homlish, had become a friend. And, as someone interested in and intrigued by the supernatural, she offered to be a researcher in the quest to find out more about the conductor.

While I explored the story talking with employees and security people in the Rubik's Cube of a building at 17th and Chew, Nancy solicited firsthand memories of encounters with "the conductor."

At first, I feared it would devolve into a story of "urban legend" dimensions. I spent considerable time at the hospital and asked several people there about the story. Somewhat understandably, employees on the job at the hospital were tightlipped about the story. A spokesman in the security department confirmed that he had heard tales about "the conductor," but dismissed them. Others I spoke to said they have had "strange feelings" in certain parts of the hospital, and had heard about "the conductor," but declined to elaborate.

Meanwhile, Nancy was gathering a thick file of testimonials from those who had seen or sensed the spirit that had etched itself into the lore of generations of workers at the hospital.

As I read the responses from real people who said they had real encounters with the sureal "conductor," I put to bed any notions of them being elements of an "urban legend," which is, by definition: *An apocryphal story involving incidents of the recent past, often including elements of humor and horror, that spreads quickly and is popularly believed to be true.*–(The American Heritage® Dictionary of the English Language).

A classic ghost story should have three complete components: (A) The "baseline," or documented incident that accounts for the imprinting of energies at a presumably haunted place; (B) The legend or legends that have grown up from that baseline; and (C) The personal experiences of individuals who have encountered the energies or entities.

The story of the conductor has all three of requirements.

The legend is decades old, and at first may seem to fall into that flimsy net I call "they say" or "it is said" stories. But, as you will soon discover, there may be a strong baseline that erases all doubt as to the veracity of those who say they have witnessed the mystery man of the old hospital.

For as long as anyone alive can remember, a story circulated in the hospital that a retired railroad conductor passed away in the hospital, and his ghost remained there. It would be described as the full apparition of an elderly man wearing a dark suit or uniform, and a train conductor's hat. Sometimes, he was seen carrying a lantern.

The phenomenon was occasionally accompanied by the opening and closing of elevator doors–with no one exiting or entering–and/or a very noticeable, unnerving, sudden, and radical change of temperature in a room or corridor.

Several nurses who worked in the 17th and Chew building were willing to share their experiences and their encounters with The Conductor, with the proviso that only their first names be given.

•

After graduating from nursing school in the mid-1980s, Vickie worked the 3 p.m. to 11 p.m. shift in the GYN Oncology Unit, then on the 5T section of the hospital. She had heard the story of The Conductor, but as a graduate nurse was usually too busy to be concerned about it.

She was working her usual shift one night, caring for one patient she remembers as being at "death's door."

Around 10 o'clock, she walked down the hallway toward the back end of the wing, toward a service elevator that was only used by hospital employees.

The night was quiet and unremarkable. And, her day's work was near an end. She was grateful that the gravely ill man had lived through her shift.

As she reached the end of the hall, she was taken aback as the service elevator doors suddenly opened. For a nervous moment, she was riveted as the elevator stood empty and the doors closed as mysteriously as they opened.

Her thoughts immediately turned to what she had heard about The Conductor. As goose bumps swept across her skin, she made her way briskly back to the dying patient's room expecting–and finding–the worst. The patient had died.

The Conductor had come to call.

In fact, he apparently came to call regularly...and often.

•

"I know he would come up and down on the back elevator at the end of 6T, the Trexler Pavilion," said Erika. "And then, there would be a death shortly after. That back elevator wasn't used by patients or families, and it was rarely used by anyone. In fact, it led to units that were closed down so there was no reason to use it. If we heard it open and no one was there, it was really scary. Why would it be stopping on our floor if no one was in it? There would always be a death shortly after."

•

A nursing supervisor at the time, Maryann was wrapping up her 3-11 shift. One night around 10 p.m., well after the 8 p.m. end of visiting hours, the patients were all sleeping and the floor was quiet.

She walked the hall one last time before the shift change and was concerned when she saw a man whom she could best describe as an older man in an old-fashioned black suit or uniform. She didn't recognize him as anyone on staff, and as there shouldn't have been any visitors there, she called out to him. She received no reply. Concerned, she approached the man but was stunned as right before her eyes, he vanished!

Maryann actually called security to report the sighting, but was simply told that she had met The Conductor.

•

Another woman who believes she had an encounter with The Conductor is Judy, who was a nursing supervisor on the night shift from 1991 to 1994.

"I would occasionally cover the 17th Street site," she noted. "As the supervisor, I would make rounds on the nursing units during the night. I was in the habit of taking the stairs throughout the hospital to save time waiting for elevators.

"One night, I finished my rounds on the 5th floor and decided to go to the supervisor's office on the second floor to work on staffing for the dayshift. There was a convenient back staircase near the kitchen, although I was not the habit of taking that particular staircase.

"As I started down, I felt suddenly that I was not alone. I felt a real chill, and the hair stood up on the back of my neck. There was a window in the staircase and I felt very frightened of that window, almost as if I knew that if I looked out that window, I would see a face (and I was on the 4th floor at the time). I felt an urgent need to get out of that staircase and I shot out the door as soon as I hit the next floor. I didn't go back on that staircase until early 2008 when I was at 17th St. for a meeting. It immediately brought back the memories of that night.

"Around the same period of time, a security guard paged me. He wanted to talk to me. He had been making his rounds in the basement. There was a room in the basement that had a door with a window that opened into a small room. The small room contained another door with a window that opened into a larger room. He opened the door to the small room, felt a chill, and looked at the door. He saw a face peering out at him. It was not a reflection of his own face. He slammed the door and ran to the nearest staircase. He was definitely scared and wanted to tell someone about his experience."

•

And then, there is Sharon, who reported several brushes with The Conductor.

While working on the renal floor and caring for a patient with uncontrollable high blood pressure. As nurses feared he may suffer a stroke, they kept a light on his room by day and night.

On routine rounds at about 2 o'clock one morning, she approached the patient's room and was shocked to see a dark figure standing at the foot of his bed. In the blink of an eye, the figure disappeared.

The next morning, the patient died.

Sharon saw the same elusive dark figure at other times–and each of those times the patient in the room where it appeared died within hours.

One event is particularly fascinating, in a morbid way.

Sharon and her cousin were both working the same shift on the same floor one night. Both women went to a gravely ill man's room to comfort him. Sharon stood at his bedside while her cousin stood at the foot of the bed.

The man, who had been moaning and groaning with pain for days, seemed contented as the two women stood by him. He asked Sharon who was there with her, standing at the foot of the bed. She told him it was her cousin, another nurse. He retorted, "No, not her...the man standing next to her, the man with the hat." Both Sharon and her cousin knew exactly who he was talking about.

Again, The Conductor had paid a visit. And again, a patient died shortly after.

•

Another nurse named Joanne related a similar, spooky story.

"When I worked on the oncology floor," she recalled, I had a patient who was dying. He was usually 'out of it,' but one night I went into his room at the end of my 3-11 shift and he was awake and talking.

"When I asked him who he was talking to, he told me he was speaking with the man in the chair who was wearing a dark coat and hat, and that the man was already dead!" Later that night, the old man followed The Conductor into the hereafter.

•

So, there they are, the legend and several personal experiences of employees of the hospital –two legs of the three needed to complete that "classic ghost story" triangle.

That third leg, the "baseline," may have been established by Nancy Homlish, who dug out a curious obituary that was printed in the *Easton Express* and *Allentown Call* newspapers.

It was the December 10, 1928 death notice of John Bright, who died in the Allentown hospital at the age of 74.

"Mr. Bright," the obituary stated, "had been admitted to the hospital five weeks ago following a stroke of paralysis."

John Bright was born in Reading but spent most of his life in Allentown. He had retired from his job four years before his death.

He was employed by the Reading Railroad company on the Allentown-Harrisburg line–as a passenger train conductor.

All aboard!

Next stop...eternity!

ENTER AS STRANGERS, LEAVE AS FRIENDS...

...OR NEVER LEAVE AT ALL!

When you walk into the Braveheart Highland Pub, you have a hard time realizing your are not among the heath, the hills, and heather, but in Hellertown.

When the present proprietors placed a proper pub within the weathered walls of what was the Hellertown Hotel, it was assumed and hoped that the ghosts of businesses past were purged from the premises.

Dramatic alterations were made on every level of the landmark building. Existing brick walls were exposed and framed with dark, rich woodwork. Scottish football posters, coats-of-arms, and artwork were mounted; the waitstaff was fitted for tartan kilts, and the menu was designed to include bridies, bangers, mince and tatties, sticky toffee pudding, and other Scottish staples.

Yes, that menu also includes the typical steak and seafood entrees of any fine restaurant, but there is a certain Aberdeen air to the Highland Pub.

Downstairs is the cozy, casual Lowland Pub; on the second floor is the lush, lavish Scotch Lounge; and on the upper floors are the living quarters of the managers and proprietors.

The Braveheart has borrowed an old Scottish phrase as its greeting:

Enter as strangers, leave as friends.

They might also appropriate another Scottish saying:

From ghoulies and ghosties and long-leggity
beasties, and things that go bump in the night,
Good Lord, deliver us!

There may be no ghoulies or long-leggity beasties at Braveheart, but there may be a few ghosties and there have been many bumps on many nights there. For, as Geddes MacGregor once wrote:

No one in Scotland can escape from the past. It is
everywhere, haunting like a ghost. To a Scot, the

past clings like sand to wet feet...the many ghosts
are always a part of them, inescapable.

Kenneth McLaughlin, general manager of the pub, said the odd and unexplainable incidents began to unfold shortly after the new owners took possession of the old hotel.

"When Robbie (Robert Millin) first moved in, quite a few things happened.

"One evening, we were on the third floor, which we had rebuilt into a place to live, and I was lying in bed with the door open, in a daze, nodding in and out of sleep.

"I woke up to go to the bathroom, and as I was getting out of bed, I saw a white figure walk past. I later asked Robbie if he had been up and about that night, and he said he had not."

Kenny described the figure as solid, but devoid of any discernible features. "When I told Robbie what I had seen," Kenny laughed, "he came over and slept in my room!"

Virtually everyone on the Braveheart staff has had encounters with the rarely seen but often sensed ghost of the pub.

"One day in the main dining room, the head chef at the time was with Robbie after closing time, winding down, and suddenly from the middle of the room they heard a loud sound of a large door closing, within about ten feet from them. The thing is, there *was* no door within ten feet of them. After that, both of them were convinced the building was haunted."

He continued, "My girlfriend and I were in bed one evening and woke up because we both heard something scratching behind the wall on the third floor. It started off on the ceiling and carried on down the wall. We had to leave the room.

"Now, that could have been a bat or a squirrel, but we didn't stay in the room long enough to think about it!"

Sensitives who have visited or worked at the pub have attributed the ghostly activity there to the presence of a woman whose spirit seems to have carte blanche to wander freely throughout the building. That her spirit is there has been determined by several "readers." Her identity remains a mystery.

It could also be that the pesky poltergeist of the pub may be rooted in a grisly discovery that was made in the hotel-to-pub transitional period.

"When the building was bought," Kenny said, "there was a semi-decomposed dead body in it. It was on the second floor, in what is now the air conditioning room. It was the body of a man."

Kenny said it had been a derelict building for several years before the new owners began the massive facelifting and renovations.

During and immediately after the period of reconstruction, other more mundane things happened, all related to the inner workings of the building.

Toilets flushed (and continue to flush) on their own. Radios played when not turned on. Mobile and landline phones either rang with no one on the other end or simply stopped operating.

"Weird, weird stuff happens here," said Justin Kline, who is another manager and resident of the pub. "One thing that constantly happens is that our light bulbs blow, sometimes one a week. And, one time, three people's cell phones all went totally blank and unusable at the exact same time. We all had to get new phones!"

Justin also said he has also heard his name called when he was absolutely certain he was alone in the building. "That has also happened many times.

"At first, it frightened me. But, I guess I have come to accept it. I live here and work here. If I'd let it bother me, I'd go out of my mind."

The discovery of the corpse on the the second floor certainly fits the profile of a possible "baseline" for the haunting of the Braveheart. Moreover, the abundance of anomalies in the building's basic systems are consistent with countless other stories where the ethereal energies of an "enchanted" place interact and interfere with the electronic and electrical infrastructure.

Early in my research into the "paranormal" and

"supernatural" (two words I abhor as I believe all of this is all quite "normal" and "natural"), I presented for anyone who cared to consider it, what I called the "rusty nail theory."

Upon death, I suggested, what was flesh and bone may become dust. But, what were electrical charges in the body's nervous system may remain as information-laden impulses which stay suspended and circulating in an eternal swirl of a magnetic field.

In my thoroughly unscholarly and unscientific proposition, could those impulses–those shards of emotions and information leftover from a life–then record themselves somehow, somewhere, on something?

As in simple video or audio recording, could not those invisible impulses become attracted to and deposited on something such as common iron oxide–rust?

Could those scientifically rational and conceivable electrical charges that burst from the corporeal confines at the time of extreme trauma–including, but not limited to, death–be the seeds of the supernatural, the pods of the paranormal?

Could those bits and pieces be put together psychically and translated as what is called a ghost?

There are two threads that weave through the

majority of tales I have investigated. Many of the "haunted" places are on or near iron ore deposits. And, many more of them have been recently renovated or altered in some way.

Could the renovations have disturbed the "recording" by exposing the rust and allowing an unwary psychic mind to push the "playback" button and detect those impulses?

As inconceivable as this may be to some, so is the proposition that living faces and forms and voices and sounds could be recorded on strips of rust-coated plastic and retrieved on a glass screen or paper speaker.

But those are the wonders we call audio and video, which in an electronic age are all so normal and natural.

And, when things go bump in the night within the walls of an old building made new again–such as the Braveheart Highland Pub, the answers to seemingly unanswerable questions may well be as scientific as they are psychic.

Gun cuireadh do chupa thairis le slainte agus sonas.

BOOKS AND BOO!

Very well, it's not very imaginative–"Books and Boo!" But, in our first *Ghost Stories of the Lehigh Valley* book, the chapter about the ghostly activity at the Easton Area Public Library was titled, "Spooks and Books." Should a third volume be necessary and should the ghosts of the library continue to tease and taunt staffers, what exceedingly clever chapter title will we come up with?

It is very likely that those ghosts will be there in the future, as they have been since the library opened in 1903. They are deeply rooted, literally and figuratively, in the soil of the library grounds.

The association that built the library purchased the land for it from the First Reformed Church. That land upon which the library was built was the city's oldest graveyard, which had reached its capacity. That should indicate where the story goes from here, and why some say the Easton Area Public Library is haunted.

The official history of the library indicates that all but a few of the more than 500 scant skeletal remains interred on the grounds were moved to other cemeteries to rest in peace. The remaining remains were gathered together and placed in a common underground vault, where they rest in pieces.

Interestingly, however, two of the more noteworthy individuals buried at the Reformed cemetery were given proper reburials on the grounds of the new library. William Parsons, one of the surveyors who laid out the town of Easton in the 1750s was given a prominent grave and marker at what is now the entrance to the library.

Elizabeth Bell Morgan (1761-1839) was reinterred beneath an ancient Indian millstone on the grounds of the library. Known in her time as "Mammy," Mrs. Morgan was a tavern owner, benefactor of a school house, and according to one historical sketch of her, "the arbiter of all disputes in Williams Township." She also dispensed legal and medical aid to anyone who came to call on her. A hill, a road, a residential community, and a golf course all carry her name.

Some believe that while Mammy's name is etched into eternity with those topographic and geographic tributes, her spirit roams the grounds of the library.

For generations, some library staff members and patrons have attributed any and all odd occurrences to Mammy Morgan's meandering ghost.

Others, however, have another idea about who

William Parsons, a surveyor who helped plan the town of Easton, is buried at the entrance to the Easton Area Public Library. The library was built atop the old First Reformed Church graveyard

haunts the library.

Henry Forster Marx was the director of the library from its opening until 1936. He put his heart and soul into the architectural appointments, operational integrity, and exterior landscaping of the library. Some of his energies and unbound loyalty to the library may remain there still today.

Barbara Wiemann, supervisor of the Local History Section of the library, tells many tales unexplainable indications that there may be a ghost in the building.

"I was working here one night and books simple fell off shelves. Now, that can happen naturally, but where they were and how they fell was not natural.

"Other staffers have felt a light breeze pass by them, and they say it's Henry, just wandering around."

Doors that creak open or closed on their own, file cabinet drawers that slide open, and the widespread sensation that an invisible entity is just out of sight, just over the shoulder of staffers and patrons are other indications that there are apparitions afoot.

Barbara added that those who believe the library is haunted also believe the epicenter of activity is a corner of the second floor where Henry Marx maintained his office.

Those believers feel that they are paying loving

The board room of the Easton Area Public Library is one of the second-floor spaces said to be visited by the ghost of a former library director.

tribute to Henry Forster Marx by arbitrarily ascribing the anomalies to him.

However, the source of the haunting may be

within the walls of that vault that lies buried beneath the back driveway.

When an addition was built alongside the original building in 1967, more bodies were found during the excavation. They were carefully retrieved and as respectfully as was possible, placed inside the old vault.

The vault itself had deteriorated, its walls crumbling and creating a sinkhole above.

"When I came to the library in 1970," Barbara Wiemann said, "the former director joked that the walls of that space were crumbling because the dead people inside it were trying to get out!"

There is a tantalizing but unsubstantiated story that has been perpetuated since the hillside was cleared in the early 20th century.

Some say the "official line" of the library is that all the graves were dutifully and diligently cleared of their contents, but that in reality, the land was simply groomed and graded right over those graves.

Absolutely not so, said Jane S. Moyer, who served as the library director from 1955 to 1976. Ms. Moyer, who lists Henry Forster Marx as her mentor, said every individual who was buried in the Reformed cemetery was properly and respectfully removed and documents on file would quickly dispel the urban legend that the graveyard was unceremoniously cleared and developed.

What's more, Ms. Moyer firmly denies the existence of ghosts at the library. But, she does believe another library in Easton is haunted–which we will learn about in another chapter.

There are others who dismiss but cannot debunk the notion of ghosts within, and without, the walls of the grand old library that overlooks the city of Easton from its prominent promontory.

But, as one staff member who declined to have her name published said, "They can say all they want. But let them be deep in the upstairs stacks and feel that puff of a breeze that ruffles your hair. Let them watch as a book slowly works its way off a shelf. Let them feel that someone was watching them, but when they'd turn around nobody would be there.

"Let those nonbelievers experience those things. I think they'd have a hard time explaining it all away. Oh, yes, the library is haunted, but not in a bad way–in a very good way."

ROAD HOUSE WRAITHS

The moment I walked into the Hanoverville Road House, all six of my senses were tweaked and teased.

The aroma of fresh food, the sight of tastefully and colorfully-appointed dining rooms, the touch of the splendid woodwork, the sound of happy customers in the bar, and the promise of the taste of Chicken Marsala, or perhaps Veal Oskar assured me I would enjoy my experience there.

Oh, yes, I did say all *six* of my senses were teased there. I had heard that spirits (other than those that lurk on shelves behind the bar) dwell within its nearly 200 year old walls. Not too many steps into the place, I and my psychically sensitive dinner date were certain that at least one permanent guest was in our midst.

Built as a commodious farmhouse in the early 19th century, the building became a stagecoach stop/general store/post office/hotel in 1837.

Through the decades, it served as a hunting lodge, family restaurant, rock music showplace, and a venue for female mud wrestling!

Several years ago, upstate New York native Charles E. Oehlbeck rescued the Road House from its wild years and established the fine "American Country Dining" restaurant that has drawn widespread praise from restaurant critics.

Accented by antiques and curiosities that range from an 1863 Springfield rifle to a collection of Mario Andretti racing memorabilia, the Road House is also graced with a substantial brick fireplace and a fine array of artwork.

It is the perfect atmosphere for an apparition or two to dwell comfortably.

Oehlbeck is not quick to admit or acknowledge that his restaurant (and residence) may be haunted. He has never personally experienced anything out of the ordinary there, but cannot dismiss reports from at least one waitress there who claims she has seen the ghost of a young boy in the main dining room after all the diners had left one night.

"There hasn't been anything really substantial here," he said, "or I would have had the Ghost Busters or Ghost Hunters in here a long time ago."

Little did he know that when my friend and I

entered the dining room without identifying ourselves, he did have "ghost hunters" in his establishment.

We spoke with the waitress who confirmed the sighting of the little boy in one corner of the dining room and talked with other staffers who said they often feel as if "someone is looking over their shoulder" there. While those sightings and sensations may be unnerving at times, they are never threatening.

Having said that, however, the energies that spiral within the comfortable confines of the Road House were strong enough to adversely affect one individual.

"We hired a waitress who worked here one day," Oehlbeck said. "After her shift she asked, 'This place is haunted, isn't it?' Well, we just kind of laughed about it, but she quit on the spot!"

He also recalled that the chap who owned the Road House before him had suspicions that it was haunted.

An initial "read" of the Road House revealed that it is the ghost of a prepubescent boy (some of the staff have dubbed him "Fred") does float across the floors and wander between–and through–the walls of the grand, old building. It may be that he was the son of someone who operated the inn in the mid-19th century, and that he passed away quietly of a childhood illness.

The intensity level of his energy is relatively low, but strong enough to easily account for reports from the past and present that quirky temperature changes and phantom breezes have been sensed by workers and patrons at the Road House.

He also seems to be largely confined to one particular section of the main dining room (seen in the photo below).

While precious little information about just who the lad may have been in life, it can be that in the afterlife he is a gentle, lonely, and somewhat forlorn spirit who is not likely to show himself as a full apparition, but more as a quiet whisper or quick wisp of air.

The Hanoverville Road House, where diners may feast on a fine selection of meals, is itself a feast for the senses–all six of them.

THE HAUNTED...
MODERN OFFICE COMPLEX

Let us first clear up some misconceptions about ghosts and hauntings.

1: The best time to hunt for ghosts is under a full moon, or on a dark and stormy night, or at the stroke of midnight.

Wrong, wrong, and wrong. Granted, the quiet and the darkness of night can intensify the imagination and make one more sensitive to the slightest aural, visual, or sensory phenomena, but it is generally accepted that neither the phase of the moon nor time of day nor meteorological conditions have any effects on where or when ghostly energies may manifest themselves.

Those energies, a.k.a. ghosts, have no calendars or clocks. They are ever-present, and are as intense at noon as they are at midnight. They don't listen to weather reports. They may be detected in fair or foul weather.

2: "I think we have a ghost in our place. But, it's a new building. Ghosts don't haunt new buildings, do they?"

Yes, they do. The energies know no chronological or architectural boundaries. Once "deposited" or imprinted on a particular spot, they remain there.

A classic story of mine in the "Ghost Stories of Berks County" trilogy involves a series of scary events inside a modern gas station/convenience store on Route 61 just north of Reading.

A clerk there informed me of the sighting of a "woman in colonial-style dress" who had been seen there by several workers, the ghostly image of an Indian some had witnessed in front of one of the coolers, and myriad phenomena that led them to believe the property was haunted.

"But, it's new store," the confused clerk said. "It can't be haunted by a woman and an Indian from the 1700s, can it?"

Yes, m'lady, it can.

When I asked her if she, or any of the other young workers there knew what stood on that site before the convenience store was built, they said no. She also admitted to never having read my first Berks County ghost book, where the story of the former building was detailed.

It was an ancient stagecoach stop and country inn, where–you guessed it–the ghost of an Indian and a colonial-era female roamed free.

That old inn was demolished to make way for the convenience store. The wrecking ball, however, could not destroy or diminish the energies that had been deposited there. That land, no matter what stands upon it, will forever remain "haunted."

This all serves as an introduction to the next Lehigh Valley ghost story, reported by a reputable individual who wishes to remain anonymous. And, just as she shall remain nameless, so shall the affected building. Let us call her "C.C.," and let us refer to the building as what it is, one of the relatively new office buildings on Highland Ave., just off Route 512 in Bethlehem.

Imagine what happened to C.C. happening to you.

"A couple of years ago, I worked the second shift in that building," C.C. said. "That meant I had to stay well after almost everyone else left the building, which was not uncommon for me.

"I worked in the training department, which was located on the second floor of the building. The room I worked in had heavy double doors that locked when shut and needed a special access card to enter. There was a side door in the area where the double doors were located, but in order to exit the door you needed to get through the double doors first, so that door was rarely used.

"One time, around 3 a.m., I was sitting alone at my desk. The lights in my area of the room were motion sensitive, so since I was sitting in the room for a period of time, the lights were off. I didn't feel uncomfortable until a very eerie feeling came over me and I heard the double doors slam shut!

"Since there was a copying machine just inside those doors, I figured that was the purpose of the person entering the room. At the time, there were only two other people in the entire building beside myself. However, they had copiers in their parts of the building, so I was confused as to why they would enter the training department for that purpose. I also thought it strange that the usual beeping sound heard when using the access card to enter the doors didn't happen.

"I called out the names of the two people I knew were in the building. No reply. I repeated it a little louder. Again, no reply. I sat very still, thinking possibly someone was playing a joke on me. Then, I said, 'Is anyone there??'

"At that very moment, I saw what looked like a child in a yellow jacket running. I was scared stiff! The lights went on. The small door to the side of that area opened and closed.

"There was no doubt in my mind then or now that someone was definitely there. I was totally creeped out!"

As C.C. tried to deal with the unsettling situation, she also tried to remain as calm as possible.

"I was in a position considered to be a role model," she continued. " I figured whoever was doing this, was not going to put one over on me.

"I also thought that if it was a child, why were they in the building, how did they get into the building, and were they OK?

"I walked cautiously to the door where I saw the child exit. That door leads to another area of the building. I walked through it–with no lights on, I might add–and called out 'IS ANYONE THERE?' I saw and heard nothing.

"I quickly left that area and went back to the double doors. I shook them to see if they would make the sound I had heard. They didn't."

C.C. had enough. "I phoned both of the people who were in the building and asked them to come to my office. I asked them if they were in my area. They both told me they weren't.

"I asked one of them to close the double doors on the other side of the hall to see if that would make them shake and make the sound I heard. It did not.

"We went together to the security area where the cameras were, and we looked in every room and hallway. We saw no one.

"We all went outside because we were smokers and needed a smoke because of how creeped out we had been."

That smoke break also cleared the air regarding

C.C.'s harrowing experience.

"When I told the other two what specifically happened, they both said, 'I'm not surprised.' I asked why they would say that. They told me that they believe the building is haunted!

"I thought they were kidding, but they were very serious. They told me a hospital for children previously stood on that site. But, none of us knew more than that."

C.C. also noted that as she told others in the building about her experiences, several said they had also felt strange sensations and seen fleeting figures of what they described as young children in the hallways and rooms.

She left that job, and the company she worked for eventually left that building. It remains to be seen, sensed, or heard whether the ghosts that C.C. and others truly believed haunted the building–er, make that *the land*–have or ever will vacate the premises.

In closing, C.C. asked what could be considered a naive but, to her, a very necessary question:

"I never repeated this story," she said, "because I didn't think anyone would believe me.

"I have been told that I have the ability to sense supernatural things. Could this be why I saw this possible spirit?"

Yes, it could, C.C., indeed it could.

CANAL TOWN POLTERGEISTS

Most folks in Freemansburg are fiercely proud and protective of their little town that clings like an appendage to the belly of Bethlehem.

The welcoming sign at the entrance to town simply states: *Freemansburg, A Canal Town.*

Indeed, Freemansburg owes much to the Lehigh Canal, which spurred growth when it was built in the 1820s. It honors that legacy with a 1.5-mile stretch of the waterway and towpath, and restored structures that include the ca. 1829 locktender's house, coal yard, grist mill, and canal lock number 44.

While it was settled in the mid-18th century, the town became an active and important "port" on the canal, which brought mills, factories, schools, churches, homes, and hotels.

One of those hotels was built by Jacob Freeman in 1830, and the village adopted his name as its name.

With all those years of history behind it, Freeman's eponymous inn had to have some mysteries, as well.

With no knowledge of any possible ghost stories there, we entered the premises and was greeted by bartender Jenny Tallarico, who had only recently taken a job there.

It wasn't long until she was introduced to the spirits that dwell there.

"I feel a presence in the basement," Jenny said. But, her experiences there have gone beyond that indefinable sensation.

"I have actually seen someone at the end of the bar," she continued. "He was just standing there, and as soon as I fixed my sights on him, he vanished. I thought I was going crazy. I asked Mike if there was anything about the place that I should know about."

Mike is the second-generation owner of the Freeman House, Mike Billetz. He broke the news to Jenny that yes, indeed, her suspicions were warranted.

"Oh yes," Mike said, "over the years there have been some occurrences here. I really don't know where to start."

As his father operated the Freeman House from the 1950s, Mike is quite familiar with the idiosyncrasies of the building. And, he has had his share of some that cannot easily be explained away.

"Most of the times, it seems like whatever spirits are in this building reside in a part of it that is usually unoccupied."

The third floor seems to be the epicenter of poltergeistic activity. "I had a few people who had stuff moved around up there," Mike added.

Most notably, one resident reported that a heavy metal closet that was in one area of a room when the left was in another area when they returned. "Nobody was ever able to explain that one," he said.

A sensitive "reader" detected spirit energy on a staircase behind the bar. She said a small, but adult figure seems to glide up and down the staircase on occasion, as if "watching over the place." And, her findings seemed to substantiate sightings that have been made there.

Mike said an apparition has been seen or sensed on that staircase. "I have actually had that feeling myself, and I feel that it is my grandfather's spirit there."

Mike's grandfather, known by his anglicized name of Thomas, emigrated from his native

Ukraine and resided for several years on the third floor of the building. "I felt a presence on the second floor landing of that staircase when I was

Does a spirit roam this staircase at the Freeman House?

in the back room, and it's hard to describe, but I felt it was my grandfather."

As for the activity on the third floor, there was one incident that not only shook Mike up, but shook him out of a good night's sleep.

He was remodeling two apartments on the third floor and living on the second floor. The living rooms of the upstairs apartments are divided by a common wall, and neither third floor apartment was occupied at the time.

"And then, one night, about 3 in the morning, I heard a loud pounding on the wall upstairs. I mean, it was loud–*bang...bang...bang!*

"Well, I thought it was my neighbor, but what would he be doing at 3 a.m., banging on the wall?

"The next day I asked him what he was doing, hanging pictures or something at 3 o'clock in the morning? He looked at me like I was crazy. He told me he heard it, too, and thought it was me banging on the wall! I never will be able to explain that one."

Could he explain it as, perhaps, a poltergeist that decided to make itself known in the wee, small hours of the morning?

"How else can I explain it? I have great respect for the spirits in here."

The Northampton County Historical Society (2008)

THE MURMURER

Nobody knows Easton like Jane Moyer knows Easton. After she retired from the Easton Area Public Library, she couldn't keep herself away from books so she soon found herself behind the desk at the Mary Illick Library of the Northampton County Historical & Genealogical Society.

Housed in two separate but connected former residences at 107 S. 4th St. in Easton, the society is the official repository for historical artifacts, documents, and books related to the history of the county.

It is also a repository for a resident ghost, according to Jane Moyer.

"We don't see it," Jane said, "but we hear it."

Jane assured me that the elusive auditory phenomenon was not a figment of one's imagination, a sound made by any kind of plumbing, mechanical, or electrical devices, or from any other identifiable source. It was not bleeding in from the outside.

"It has to be a quiet morning," she continued. "I would come in around eight in the morning, I'd be alone in the building, and I would hear it.

"There are two buildings here. One is called the Illick House and one is the Mixsell House.

"I would come in through the Illick House and then open the door that goes into the Mixsell House. Many a morning I would go into the Mixsell House and I would stand at the foot of the steps and I would hear a murmuring sound coming from upstairs, on the second floor.

"The first time I heard it, I called out, figuring someone was in the building. Of course, nobody answered. One day I actually went upstairs, but there was nobody there."

Jane can never decipher any words or phrases or determine if the murmuring was from a male or female, young or old, English or foreign language.

"But," she insisted, "you can hear voices,

people talking. It sounds like at least two people up there. And, several of us have heard it."

The murmuring ghost–and Jane truly believes it is a ghost–remains a morsel of mystery in that haven of history.

Jane Moyer is quite comfortable around spirits. When asked if she believes in ghosts, her answer is decisive: "Oh, of course, I have a ghost in my house!"

She lives in a ca. 1930 home in Forks Township, and she believes that house is enchanted by a very special ghost.

"I raise dogs," she noted. "And, about a week after my husband died, my one Irish Setter was at the foot of the steps. She was wagging her tail and whimpering as I watched her from the kitchen.

"I went over to her and watched as she put her head down and walked away. I saw her do that several times.

"Now, was she hearing or seeing somebody? I don't know. But, I really believe she felt something and it was the spirit of my husband."

In her position as the librarian at the Historical Society, Jane comes into contact with many people with old properties that harbor legends and unanswered questions. Sometimes, the questions involve ghostly activity. She has a wonderful attitude about how folklore and history can be compatible and why many of the old buildings in and around Easton and the Lehigh Valley may be haunted by those who lived in them long ago.

"I think old houses have feelings in them that don't always disappear as they get new tenants," she suggested. "I think those feelings–those spirits–linger in those old houses."

Colleen Cunningham Lavdar is the executive director of the historical society, and she is also convinced that one of the society's permanent exhibits...so to speak...is its ghost.

Ms. Lavdar said,"When I first started here, that very first day, as everyone was leaving the building, I asked 'Is there anything I need to know about these buildings?'

"They asked, 'like what?' I said, 'Well, like, are there any ghosts here that I need to be aware of?'"

That opened the doors...so to speak.

Everyone summarily dismissed Colleen's question–everyone but Jane Moyer.

"Jane said to me that she wasn't going to tell me there were ghosts here. I would have to find out for myself," Colleen said.

"Jane told me that I would hear footsteps, I would hear voices...and left it at that."

And, it wasn't long until Colleen did hear the footsteps, the voices, and the murmuring.

Several of her experiences in the building,

however, transcended the auditory sensations that she had been warned about.

When giving a tour in the Military Room on the second floor of the museum, she was explaining the uniforms and artifacts in a display that included a "draft wheel," a cylindrical device used to select numbers for drafting men into the military during the Civil War.

"When I give tours, very often people will ask if there are any ghosts here. My response is to ask them if they believe in ghosts. If they say yes, I'll tell them that they just might find some spirits here."

It was in front of that military display when one young visitor popped the question. He might have gotten an instant, vivid answer.

"Right after the question about ghosts was asked," the society director said, "the draft wheel started spinning!"

Colleen said she is comfortable in the building. "There's never a bad feeling here. It's definitely not a place you have to be afraid of.

"The ghostly activity here has just become a fact of life."

...so to speak.

[Author's Note: By the time this book is published, the buildings mentioned in this story may have become an historic house museum, as the society was scheduled to move its museum into its new headquarters in the "Sigal Building" at 342 Northampton Street in Easton]

The Hotel Bethlehem

HAUNTED BETHLEHEM

Its downtown is one of the most lovely of any city in Pennsylvania. Its institutes of higher learning are among the most respected in the United States.

Bethlehem is charming. It is historic. And, it is haunted–quite haunted.

In my first volume of Lehigh Valley ghost stories, I highlighted several hauntings in Bethlehem. And, when I sought updates and additions for this edition, I found that the ground had already been plowed by a friend and colleague.

Katherine Ramsland and I have crossed paths and shared thoughts at several paranormal conferences over the years, and she agreed to share information she and co-author Dana DeVito gleaned for their 2007 book, *Bethlehem Ghosts: Historical Hauntings In & Around Pennsylvania's Christmas City.*

That book was published by Second Chance Publications, owned by Carol and Mark Nesbitt, who operate the original ghost tours in Gettysburg and are also friends and veterans of the paranormal conference trail.

Dr. Ramsland, professor of forensic psychology at DeSales University and author of 33 books, including *Ghost: Investigating the Other Side,* has an impressive body of work that includes bestsellers dealing with vampires, witches, and serial killers. She told me it was the blend of history and mystery in Bethlehem that drove her to research the ghosts of her adopted home town.

"When Dana DeVito and I decided to write a book about hauntings specific to Bethlehem," she said, "we found that many businesses along Main Street had associated ghost stories. In fact, right there in the Moravian Book Shop that Dana managed was an interesting tale, told to her by a night supervisor."

The Moravian Book Shop

Much more than a book shop, the store is also home to one of the most popular places in town to enjoy a bite to eat.

"Food is prepared in the kitchen for the deli, both of which are closed an hour before the rest of the store closes," Katherine continued, "and this duty falls to the kitchen crew. But one evening, a supervisor was walking around closing the place.

"The doors were locked and all the customers were gone. She noticed a figure in the back hallway, moving toward the kitchen, so she followed it into the kitchen. Although no one was there, and there was no way out, she noticed that the burners had been left on.

"Since it's not her job to check this area, without this figure, she would have left the store and there was every possibility it might have started a fire. She turned off the burners and left the place as fast as she could. The staff decided that the 'ghost' had been protecting them."

One of my favorite stops during any of my shopping trips to Bethlehem is Donegal Square, an Irish/Celtic shop and tea room. Katherine Ramsland discovered that there was a *boo* or two in the charming store.

"A story I heard when I first moved to Bethlehem," she said, "was from Donegal Square, run by Neville Gardner, and he repeated it for Dana and me."

The following is Mr. Gardner's story, as told to Katherine and Dana:

Over the past 12 years since I bought our building at 534 Main Street," he said, "we have had many odd things happen of a supernatural

Donegal Square

nature. The first really noticeable event occurred the night before we opened our tea room in September 1997. I got a call at 6:00 a.m. from a worker in the kitchen who reported that when she came into the kitchen, she found water coming through the ceiling from the apartment above.

I got dressed and raced in to check it out. Upstairs, in the unoccupied space above the kitchen, the whole place was saturated, but with no evidence of water running anywhere. The carpets were so wet they squished when I walked on them. The doors and windows were all secure, and there was no logical reason why the place was wet. I went into the bathroom opened the drawers under the vanity and found them full of water to the brim. It was really strange. I never did figure out where the water came from and this incident never happened again.

"But there were others," Katherine continued. "Neville had once told me about finding a tunnel behind the store during renovations, and after opening it, there were several incidents."

Again, Neville Gardner's words:

Our apartment on the second floor above Donegal Square had a bedroom in which apparently something strange happened on a regular basis. During the night, if a guest was sleeping in that bed, they reported feeling something get into bed beside them. This was apparently a pretty frequent and scary event. Other tenants have told stories as well. One tenant told us that one New Year's Eve in their lounge area, they heard a champagne cork pop and heard violin music. They even smelt cigar smoke, but when they opened the door, nobody was there.

We believe the activity is due to some energy form lingering in this dimension from something that happened in the past. Perhaps it could be something to do with the Marquis de Lafayette, who was nursed back to health in the location where our building now stands after he sustained an injury during the Revolutionary War. The story goes that the daughter of the property own took care of him and he may have fallen in love with her. The Marquis returned to France shortly afterward and perhaps the young woman died an unquenched passion that resulted in the energy that dwells in the building to this day.

Katherine and Dana also found a Bethlehem theater that presented more than cinematic shows within its walls.

"Just off Main Street, on Broad," Katherine told me, "is the Boyd Theater, one of the more interesting movie theater experiences in the region. It opened on September 1, 1921 as the Kurtz Theater, featuring silent motion pictures and vaudeville acts. Reportedly, the figure of a woman from Victorian times has been spotted here, and some think she's the same one who's associated with the Wachovia Bank building down the street. Supposedly, when that building was a nightclub, a murder happened there, and some people claim to have seen a female ghost.

"So, I arranged to meet two friends to go see a movie at the Boyd in December 2007. When I arrived, I asked the girls behind the ticket counter if they'd ever seen the ghost there, and they gave me one of those looks that all ghost hunters know...'Yeah, right.' Then I went in and found that one of my friends had arrived before me, and she seemed disturbed about something. She told me that she had just gone in to the auditorium and in an area of seats across the large space, where no one else was sitting, she saw a woman she thought was me. The woman turned and waved to her and while it was too dark to see clearly, my friend assumed I had found a seat and was beckoning her over. She glanced back into the lobby to see if the third member of our party was coming, and when she looked at the seats again to find 'me,' no one was there. That's when I arrived. She told me her experience and I learned that she hadn't then realized there was a female ghost in the Boyd. Now she does."

A veritable epicenter of ghostly activity in downtown Bethlehem, and what Katherine considers to be the most haunted building on Main Street is the Hotel Bethlehem.

"I had already heard that the third floor was haunted by a suicide victim who had jumped out a window back in the 1950s or 1960s. Supplies disappear and appear again in odd places, and several of the staff claim to have seen apparitions.

"I worked with the hotel's historian to find out what I could about its long history and we discovered a host of unique stories about the building that could explain some of the hauntings. We learned about a man named Frank Smith, who'd had a partnership associated with Bethlehem Steel. He was in financial difficulty, and in his office on the third floor he apparently shot himself with a .357 magnum. Supposedly his ghost wanders that floor, making noises, and one worker reported seeing the figure of a gentleman in a suit, in the same bathroom where Smith had died, and this figure had disappear right in front of her.

"On this same floor, people have reported the loud crash of weights dropping in the fitness area, when it's locked and no one's inside. Apparently, this has been a common complaint. In addition, the image of a little girl was once seen after hours in the window of this room, from the street outside.

"The night engineer also told me a few stories, one of which occurred on the third floor. He was walking down the hall one night near the fitness room when he saw the image of a tall woman wearing a sweater and gray pants looking at him through the glass door, from inside the room. He had just locked it and no one had been in there, but there she was, staring right at him.

He decided to just walk away.

"However, it's Room 932 that appears to generate the most tales. One couple claimed to have encountered a man in his underwear who'd said, 'You're in my room, please leave,' so they did. But there was no other guest checked into that room. The other was of a young woman who had stepped out of the shower of the newly-renovated bathroom and saw the reflection of a man in the mirror. He'd walked away from her and disappeared. She went to the desk to report this, but when that staff checked they found that no one else was in the room. A few of us have spent the night in there, and we report on that in *Bethlehem Ghosts*."

THE BARN

Jill Stefko has been interested in and investigating haunted places for decades, and her native Bethlehem and Northampton County soil has been fertile hunting grounds for her paranormal pursuits.

Long before ghost hunting and the documentation thereof became as widespread as it is today, Jill and a handful of others in the Lehigh Valley were out there, seeking the supernatural.

She recalled her first venture to what she was told was a haunted barn in Fountain Hill.

It was a warm day in September, 1965 when she and a friend parked a few hundred yards away from the barn and walked toward it. As they approached the building, they were greeted by a startling sight.

"We were walking on the sidewalk when my friend suddenly grabbed my arm," Jill recalled. "She was very upset and pointed to something on the ground. A dead raven. She is part Hungarian and also has Gypsy blood. She told me that the raven was a bad omen."

Near the barn was a construction site that was buzzing with activity. The sound of the construction work was hardly the atmosphere for a ghost hunt.

"When we got to the barn, the huge door was open, so we walked in. We were only about two or three feet from the door. The air was much cooler in the barn. We could no longer hear the noises from the construction workers.

"What we did hear was voices telling us to get out. My friend and I exchanged puzzled glances. We did the logical thing. We went out of the barn.

"We talked a bit, then decided to go back into the barn. The same thing happened. So, we intrepid ghost hunters left."

Jill's indefatigable penchant for the pairing of history and the paranormal led her to become a pioneer in the field of ghost tours.

"In 1998, I created walking ghost tours of historic Bethlehem in conjunction with the

Bethlehem Tourism Authority (BTA). I worked with the executive director, Mary Ann Dwyer and other wonderful people.

"We had two very successful years with the tours. But, when the BTA was disbanded in 2000 by the mayor at that time, the ghost tours were also discontinued."

The tours stepped off from the old Visitors Center and every effort was made to create a mood for the moment. The starting point was accented with Halloween decorations and eerie music. The guides wore cloaks and carried candles and lanterns.

While the tours focused mainly on the historic district of the city, Jill figured she could include her experience of the disembodied voices in Schwab's barn as an anecdotal addendum to her spiel on the tours.

"Well," she said, "I had a true story and I had an audience. And, Charlie Schwab was a part of Bethlehem's history."

Indeed, Charles M. Schwab was the founder of Bethlehem Steel, patron of the city's legendary Bach Choir, civic leader, and philanthropist whose largesse extended far beyond the Lehigh Valley.

"Schwab was also human," Jill Stefko noted. "He was a gambler, union buster and businessman of questionable tactics. The 1929 stock market crash ruined Schwab financially. He died bankrupt in 1939."

On a V.I.P. preview night of the tours, one of the guides surprised Jill by asking if he could relate a short ghostly connection from his childhood.

"Retired radio personality Alan Raber, who was a tour guide, asked me if he could tell the story of Charlie Schwab's barn. Of course he could! Then, he told me that when he was a boy, and he and his mother would go by the barn, she would say to him, 'That's Charlie Schwab's barn. It's haunted.'"

And, of course the "rest of the story" is that the barn that Jill and her friend had their creepy encounter was the Schwab barn, which has since been demolished.

The flamboyant Charlie Schwab was from Cambria County, Pennsylvania and resided in mansions there and in Manhattan. He actually spent relatively little time in Fountain Hill.

Jill did not and could not directly link Charlie Schwab with any haunting in or around Bethlehem.

Interestingly, though, a building at 114 W. Fourth Street in the city has an association with Schwab and spirits.

I attempted to retrieve that story from the owners of a restaurant that occupied that site. But, upon my arrival at the building, I discovered I was too late–the restaurant had closed.

But, Jill remembered the story from her ghost hunting days.

"Anna Mia's was an excellent Italian restaurant. The building is haunted and the restaurant owners liked their "friendly" ghost.

"People heard inexplicable music when no radio was playing. Employees on the second floor witnessed footsteps and voices downstairs, but when they checked, no one was there.

"Objects moved and some securely hung on walls fell. There were no reports of anyone ever actually seeing ghosts. Prior to being a restaurant, it was Cantelmi's Funeral Home. At one time Charlie's in-laws owned the Fourth Street building, and he and his wife stayed there before moving into their new house."

The *name* of Charles M. Schwab is, ironically, connected to one building in, of all places, State College, Pennsylvania. But, the ghost there is generally regarded to be that of former Penn State University president George. W. Atherton, who is buried adjacent to the structure.

According to sources at PSU, some actors and patrons of the Schwab Auditorium believe it may be the auditorium's benefactor, Charlie Schwab (the ghost has actually been jokingly referred to as "Schwaboo"), but most speculate it is President Atherton, just rising from his grave to enjoy a show.

Jill Stefko has appeared on radio talk shows and has offered her insight on the unseen in several venues.

She has been interviewed by students in a journalism class at Lehigh University, and subjected to incisive questions.

"One time," she recalled, "I was asked what I say to skeptics about the reality of paranormal things.

"My answer was that I do not have to prove things exist. Prove to me that these things *do not* exist."

[Author's Note: The photograph of the barn at the beginning of this chapter is for illustration purposes only. It is not the old Schwab barn, but in fact a haunted barn near Nashville, Tennessee. And, the Charles M. (Charlie) Schwab referred to in this story is no relation to the Charles R. (Chuck) Schwab, founder of Charles Schwab & Co. investment corporation.]

Stemie's Place: The former Black Horse Inn.

THE GANGLAND GHOST

Be it on a dark night or a gray, gloomy day, the serpentine Route 611 cuts an sinuous course as it snakes from Easton and south along the Delaware River.

In the wedge between road and river is an inn that has been catering to weary, hungry, and thirsty travelers since 1782. Privileged and poor have supped and stayed there. Untold stories are locked within its thick fieldstone walls.

One of those tales reads like a script from a Hollywood gangster movie–but it is all very real. It is the story of a prohibition-era mob "hit" that has become a cold case–a very cold case.

And, the "wise guy" who was whacked has haunted the building since he fell in a hail of gunfire in the summer of 1928.

They called him "Johnny the Wop." He called himself Johnny Farrara. But, it's believed his real name was Saverio Damiano. And, it is further believed that he was "connected" with a widespread network of organized crime figures in New York, New Jersey, and Pennsylvania.

It was said that Johnny was at the Black Horse Tavern to "visit" with a stunning blonde woman who was staying there. That stunning blonde, however, was the girlfriend of a rival mobster back in New York.

Word got out that Johnny the Wop was carrying on with the mobster's woman, and it was believed that a "hit" was put out him. According to contemporary reports, Max Shimkovitz, then the proprietor of the tavern, took a call from a mysterious man and relayed a baneful message: "Johnny," he warned, "they are coming over tomorrow night."

Johnny took a drag on his cigar, slugged another shot of Scotch, and replied, "Let 'em come, Max, let 'em come."

They came. They cornered Johnny. They gunned him down as he was on the telephone just inside the front door.

The phone was located next to the door that opened to the stairway to the cellar. Maybe he had ducked inside the door so he could hear his phone conversation, or maybe his assailants cornered him into the stairway. For whatever reason he was there, it was down those steps that Johnny's bloody, bullet-riddled body tumbled.

The four gangsters who burst into the bar that night left no clues. They came, they killed, and they disappeared into the night.

Given the circumstances at that particular time and at that particular place, the proprietor was less than enthusiastic about calling the cops in after the murder.

After all, it was Prohibition, and the Black Horse was, in the vernacular of the day, a speakeasy. A report at the time noted that responding officers found "plain evidences of a disorderly house with liquor and beer on sale and slot machines in the middle of the barroom." But, they were concerned with something much bigger than some illegal booze and one-armed bandits.

Investigators corralled nine witnesses, but none could provide any substantive information. It was determined that when he was shot, Johnny was on the phone with Sam Scallesi, an Allentown man who was under indictment for the bombing of the home of a Hazleton policeman. Questions were asked, leads were followed, but they all led to dead ends.

From the day of his demise through the decades since his still-unsolved murder, Johnny the Wop has haunted the building. And, he is still very active at times.

When Alfred Stempo bought the former Black Horse Tavern in 2002, he was well aware of Johnny's story and his and other ghosts that are said to haunt the place.

And, it didn't take long until he got his first clue that an unseen entity may rule the roost in the historic old hotel that was built during the Revolutionary War years.

Al's sister-in-law had come to call shortly after he took possession of the building and business, which he renamed "Stemie's Place." She brought her rather sturdy Doberman with her. From the moment the woman and her dog entered the place, the Doberman appeared a bit nervous. He wandered up the staircase, and when he reached the top, he turned around awkwardly and bolted down the steps and out the building.

"We never figured out what that was all about," Al said. But, it generally regarded that the dog was spooked by the spirits that dwell there.

Also early into his ownership of the building, Al was greeted with yet another "sign."

One day, he walked alone through the building and went *mano-a-mano* with the manifestations. Aloud, he warned the ghosts that if they dared to trifle with him, he'd call a priest in to get rid of them. The response was an eye opener.

"Well, right after I said that," Al recalled, "I heard all kind of noises–whooshing sounds, banging sounds. I guess the ghost didn't appreciate my threat."

Al is a tough-talking kind of guy, but always ready with a rapid-fire witticism. Firm and fair, the veteran restaurateur knows how to deal with people in the real world–and does his level best to handle those in the netherworld.

"Hey," he laughed, "don't forget, I'm a pure Slovak. I'm one with the gypsies. I was raised with that sort of stuff."

Al holds dear to him his family's heritage of superstition and tradition. "We have one interesting old tradition," he noted. "A few days before somebody dies, they see 'the man.' In my own family, we have had loved ones speak of seeing 'the man,' and within two or three days, they died."

This may be why Al Stempo is at once philosophical and feisty regarding the resident ghosts at Stemie's Place. "I figure a ghost can't hurt you if you're not afraid of it," he stated. I'm always looking for an explanation. I always have to find out why things happen."

Al Stempo probes the stairs where "Johnny the Wop" was murdered in a 1928 "underworld feud."

That is more easily said than done, as Al has discovered.

Waitresses, bartenders, and Al's wife, Maria, are among the legion of employees and patrons who have reported ghostly activity.

"Things were flying around in the kitchen for awhile," he said. "A butter knife soared from one shelf to another, about four feet away.

"A waitress was doing her thing in the ladies room one time, and said she saw the legs of a man walking back and forth on the other side of the stall. There was no man in the ladies' room at that time. She was freaked out."

A utility repairman was once so traumatized while working in the basement that he abruptly and rudely left the job undone, stalked out of the building in a perceived panic, and never returned.

The steps that Johnny the Wop fell to his death on are still there, but rarely used. No one is comfortable in the basement. Those steps and that subterranean chamber appear to be the epicenter of the energies that spiral through the building.

On a particularly busy day at the tavern not long ago, the ghosts were also particularly busy. Items fell off shelves or went missing. Strange incidents seemed to impact everyone who was working there that day.

"Finally," Al said, "I yelled out– 'cut it out, Johnny! I don't need this s - - - today!"

At that moment, Al and a waitress heard a thumping, tumbling sound on the basement steps. A later check revealed that nothing had fallen down on them.

"Sometimes," Al laughed, "maybe you're

better off not disturbing something."

Heather Smedley is a self-confessed "river rat" who has worked her way up the Delaware River valley working as a bartender at several haunted inns, including New Hope's legendary Logan Inn. She also considers herself to be sensitive to supernatural forces. So, getting a job at Stemie's and finding out it was haunted was no big deal.

Heather said there is an ever-present, sometimes overpowering feeling that sweeps through the building. "The attic is very, very bad," she said. "But, it's all over. It's nothing evil, but it is very noticeable."

On several occasions, unsuspecting patrons have crossed paths with the ghosts of Stemie's.

"I was standing next to a guy and his wife, talking at the bar," Al recalled. "The guy took two steps forward and nodded his head. I asked him what he was doing.

"He said, very seriously, that he had let 'that guy' go by. He acted as if I was crazy because I asked him. Well, his wife and I looked at him and asked, 'What guy?' He was annoyed, and said, 'The guy who just went through here!'"

Al said the man became almost belligerent, insisting someone had just walked through their little grouping and none of the others had seen him. Al insisted it was not a joke or a stunt. The man went as far as to describe the man who passed by, and Al went as far as to look around the restaurant and bar for a man fitting that description, but found no one.

You may have noticed references to "ghosts," as in the plural, at Stemie's. That's because it is believed that while Johnny the Wop is the "Type A" spirit there, other entities are active.

Two Indian children are buried on the property, and when Al took over the business he was told that their ghosts have been seen and felt in the building.

And, a dearly beloved waitress and friend of Al and Maria died on the job in the tavern. "She's here," he affirms, "and I know that. Every once in a while we will smell her perfume. She is definitely here with us."

Maria Stempo has sensed the spirit in several areas of the restaurant. "From what we understand from older customers," she said, "former owners here were actually chased out by the ghosts. It really doesn't bother me," she said.

There are many mysteries there that may never be solved. There is a small, inaccessible room that can be discerned from the outside but is behind tightly sealed walls on the inside. Al would love to open that space and see what may be inside.

Making that prospect even more tantalizing is

the age-old rumor that Johnny the Wop stashed a pile of cash somewhere in the old building and that his ghost remains there to protect his booty.

Another legend has it that Johnny's ghost is on an eternal vigil, waiting to gain revenge should his killers ever return to the tavern.

"Stemie" has grown comfortably within the decidedly haunted walls of his "place."

"A lot of people have come in here and have wanted to have seances and raise the spirits," he said. "I say no. Leave the ghosts alone."

He would like that to be a two-way street. But, he has had to face reality.

Since he reopened the business, he has been set back by floods and fires that have threatened its existence. Some people have blamed the ghosts for the setbacks.

Al doesn't necessarily subscribe to that theory, but in his characteristically ebullient way, he did throw up his hands in frustration one time and call out to whomever–wherever–may be listening.

"Hey, I said out loud to the ghosts. I'm giving you heat. I'm giving you air conditioning. I've giving you a nice place here. So leave me alone! I'm trying to run a business here. You're killin' me!"

Trailing off in laughter and shrugging his shoulders, Al quipped, "Hey, I figure a ghost can't hurt you if you're not afraid of it."

CREEKSIDE CREEPS

Does a ghost prowl and protect the Creek Road mansion known traditionally as the "Riegel House?"

On looks alone, the stately mansion owned by Lehigh University "looks haunted." And, an area historian said it just may be.

Lee A. Weidner has authored numerous articles and books about history in the Hellertown and Lower Saucon areas. When approached about ghost stories in his neck of the woods, he cited the Leithsville Inn, a certain grist mill, and the Riegel House.

"As kids, we were told to not even look at that house when we went past it," he said. "There were all kinds of rumors and stories about that place. Some said it was a house of ill-repute, and others said it was haunted.

"It was called 'The House of Seven Gables'–although are more than seven gables. But mostly, it was called the 'haunted house.'"

Weidner cannot substantiate any hauntings there, but has heard through the folklore grapevine that the resident wraith of the Riegel House is a Revolutionary War soldier who inhabits a sub-basement and has been known to amble between the mansion and the Lime Kiln Burial Ground, just up the road.

THE PHANTOM FLIRT

We met Colleen Cunningham Lavdar a few pages back when she gave us her take on the haunting of the Mixsell House, which at the time of this writing was the headquarters of the Northampton County Historical & Genealogical Society.

As executive director of the society, Ms. Lavdar is immersed in local history. Professionally, she travels on that broad, bright boulevard of history. Personally, she likes to take an occasional turn onto the dimly-lit, narrow lanes of legend and lore.

A story she is particularly intrigued by is one that dates to the Colonial era and has been told and retold by generations of storytellers and writers.

It was attributed to Elizabeth F. Ellet, a poet and writer who traveled in elite literary circles of the mid 19th century. A prolific author of books and articles, Mrs. Ellet published the following story in the wildly popular *Godey's Lady's Book*.

It is the story of a horrible crime that may well have left an eternal imprint in a certain neighborhood of the city.

I, too, like a juicy legend. And, the story as related by Mrs. Ellet is about as juicy as a 19th century story can get. Cheating husbands, jealous wives, sex, murder, a ghost–is that enough juice for you? Keep reading.

On that boulevard of real history, it is noted that there was a documented witchcraft trial in Pennsylvania (see "The Black Arts and 'Imaginary Crimes'" chapter in *Ghost Stories of Chester County and the Brandywine Valley*, Exeter House Books, 2001).

On that dark lane of legend, there is Elizabeth Ellet's "The Fate of a Flirt of the Olden Times."

Perhaps it was written to serve as a morality lesson or social commentary. Perhaps it was "ripped from the headlines" of the 18th century day and has strong roots in reality.

The cast of characters includes a woman referred to as "Mrs. Winton," her husband, said to be a member of the Colonial Assembly; several married men and their wives, who, in the writer's words, "stayed at home, read the Bible, and wore frocks."

The couples in question were simple folk. The Easton of the day was a small river town where everyone knew everyone.

So, when several wagons pulled up to a small but handsome empty house on the edge of town, it was cause for serious scrutiny.

It became quickly obvious that these were "city folk" moving in. Their fancy furniture, their waves of tradesmen, and their overall "English" look drew the attention of the largely Germanic populace.

The women of the community especially examined the appearance and comportment of the woman of the house.

"At the first glance," the story noted, "one could not but acknowledge her singular beauty. Her form was faultless in symmetry...the complexion being of a clear brown, set off by luxuriant black hair, and a pair of brilliant eyes."

And, oh yes, the men of Easton also took note of her charms.

Shortly after the couple moved into the house, the gentleman left town, presumably to tend to his political responsibilities in Philadelphia.

Mrs. Winton tried to assimilate into Easton society. She found out soon that it was a rather closed society, and also discovered that while the women greeted her with suspicious smirks, the men went out of their way with courtesies.

What was the gossip of loose-lipped ladies took a terrible turn when two or three of them decided to find out if what they had suspected might be true.

Sure enough, one early evening in the woods behind a popular pond used by young people for fishing and swimming, Mrs. Winton was spied arm-in-arm with the husband of one of the voyeurs.

Enraged, the women gathered after dark to plot their response to the tart's tempting of that man, and what they feared were many other husbands of town.

Every wife was certain that their husband had availed himself of her "hospitality." Crafting masks they affixed to their faces, the women hastened to the home of the hussy. They would punish her for her improprieties.

They reached the house and found her there with her young son. One of the women grabbed the boy and took him away to an undisclosed location. The others massed around Mrs. Winton, gagged her, and dragged her to the pond. The story then got very interesting:

"Then each, in turn, seizing her enemy by the shoulders, plunged her in, head and all, crying as she did so, 'This is for my husband!' 'And this for mine!' 'This for mine!' was echoed, with plunges, in quick succession, till the work of retribution was accomplished and the party hurried to shore."

Something stirred in the woods, and the women scattered, leaving Mrs. Winton on the shore of the pond.

They were sure they had taught her a wet

lesson and left her tortured, but alive, as they rushed to their homes.

It was a type of torture that could be traced nearly a century before that night in the mid-18th century. It was a variation of the "ducking stool" punishment doled out to suspected witches and women of ill-repute.

When the sun came up the next day, it shone on the shore of the pond and the rumpled, lifeless form of Mrs. Winton. Unbeknownst to the vigilante wives, their victim had been drowned during their frenzied feast of hatred.

Shocked, the women rallied together secretly and closed their ranks. Never would they admit to their complicity, and never would any other perpetrator be penalized for it. The murder of Mrs. Winton remained unsolved.

Not long after the hideous incident, sightings of a ghostly woman were reported from at the site of the crime.

The pond was drained, the woods were cleared, and a stable was built on the reclaimed land.

Mrs. Ellet was personally acquainted with the owner of the stable. She wrote, "I have heard him relate how one of his servants, who had never heard the story, had rushed in one night, much alarmed, to say that he had seen a female figure, in old-fashioned cap and white gown, standing at the door of the stable."

Other people–young and old, male and female, humble and haughty–told of a mysterious woman who wandered aimlessly in the area where the pond once stood.

"Another friend who resides near," Mrs. Ellet noted, "was told by his domestic that a strange woman had stood at the back gate, and had suddenly disappeared when asked who she was.

"Thus there seems ground enough to excuse the belief, even now prevalent among the common people in Easton, that the spirit still walks at night about that portion of the town."

Elizabeth Ellet wrote her story about the "flirt" in the 19th century. The incident took place in the 18th century.

In the 21st century, does the phantom of the flirt still wander at the sites of the old pond, or her old house?

In the course of researching information for this book, I had been told that a good ghost story was to be found at the First Presbyterian Church on Spring Garden Street in Easton.

A call to Rev. Charles F. Holm confirmed that there was a ghost story there, and–*voila!*–the ghost was none other than Mrs. Winton, a.k.a. "The Flirt."

The setting of the story isn't actually the sanctuary, but a former church property just down the street at 4th and Spring Garden.

"It's a really fascinating story," Rev. Holm said. "It's wonderful–about the life and times in Easton in those times. And, how 'different' people were either accepted or rejected by the community."

According to legend, the old Presbyterian Manse, or minister's house at 4th and Spring Garden, was haunted by the ghost of the woman who was tortured to death by the jealous women.

Several members of the church congregation reported seeing the figure of a forlorn female gliding through the old parsonage, which was vacated by the church in 1926 and incorporated about twenty years later into the former Churchman's Business School building. The minister's house still exists there, and the church has recently used it for special functions.

The business school closed in 2004, and at the time of the writing of this book, the building was scheduled to be renovated into a mixed-use complex which would include residences, offices, and a restaurant.

Will the ghost of "the flirt" continue to inhabit the restored building? Remember–according to all that has been learned about "hauntings," the energy remains imprinted and remains no matter what is built on or around it.

Rev. Holm speculated that after the tortured

woman's horrible death, her spirit found peace.

"Maybe," he said, "she was looking for a friendly place and she chose to remain in the minister's house."

Or, perhaps her tormented ghost is bound to the spot where she died and where her body was found.

Historians believe that the pond where "the flirt" died was on a site now occupied by the *Express-Times* newspaper offices.

So, is the newspaper building haunted by the hussy? Does her sad spirit still stroll the place where her life was so cruelly taken?

We'll let the newspaper investigate and report on that.

(EDITOR'S NOTE: Another version and additional information and attribution regarding the ghostly activities in the former parsonage of the church is available in "Ghost Stories of the Lehigh Valley," book one.)

THE PLAYFUL WAIF OF THE BUCKEYE TAVERN

Dear Mr. Adams:
I would like to know if you have ever heard of the Buckeye
Tavern in Macungie as being haunted.
We were having dinner one night in the dining area with the
fireplace, near the bar. My back was to the bar area and I felt
someone or something tug, or a better word might be *yank* my hair
from behind.
The woman with us said she saw my head yank back a little and
asked if I was OK...It was pretty weird. I'm all about spirits, ghosts,
etc., and that was probably the first time anything like that had ever
happened to me.

With that email from a correspondent I shall
identify only as "D.W.," my quest began for more
information about a possible ghost story at the
venerable Macungie restaurant.

Venerable? While it has operated under its

current name only since 1987, the building has served patrons since 1768. There have been many renovations and additions made to the Brookside Road landmark. But, the core structure remains, and within it may be a ghost or two.

"There supposedly is the ghost of a little girl here," said manager Waynette Nothstein.

While she has never witnessed a full apparition, Waynette confirmed that strange things occasionally happen there. "I have seen things moving out of the corner of my eye when nobody else is here," Waynette continued. "And, several of us have heard weird sounds."

Waynette has worked at the Buckeye for 13 years, but her connection there goes farther back than that. In the 1970s, when it was a pub called "The Load of Mischief," she actually taught disco dancing in the second floor room where the little girl has been seen.

She has been seen by passersby, neighbors, and Buckeye customers (*before* imbibing in the other kind of spirits there). They have reported the face of a quizzical, innocent little girl peering down from a second floor window on the Brookside Road side of the building.

But, D.W.'s email added a new dimension to the account of the little girl.

A trusted "sensitive" individual who had no knowledge whatsoever about the story of the little girl visited the Buckeye for dinner one evening. She did not identify herself as a "ghost hunter," but that is exactly why she was there.

She reported back to me that as soon as she entered the building she felt a very noticeable presence.

"From what I could gather psychically," she said, "there seems to be at least two spirits there. One is an elderly male who actually, for some reason, is on the walkway between the big parking lot and the front door. I felt his spirit close to what I guess is the kitchen door on the side of the building.

"What anyone dining there would probably notice, is a very young, female ghost whose energy seems to ramble wherever it wants.

"I would describe her as being maybe five or six years old when she passed. I also have the feeling that she is not caucasian. She may be a little black girl, or even a Native American."

Although she admitted it was all psychic speculation, our medium friend further described the Buckeye's most active spirit as playful, "waif-like," and probably about the height of the back of one of the chairs.

And, that's just about the right height to tug the hair of an unsuspecting customer–like D.W.!

...or you!

TALES OF CORPSE HOUSES, CRICKETS OF DEATH, AND GIRLS WHO TURN INTO SNAKES

Long before the mega-malls and "lifestyle centers," the world-class festivals and fairs; and well before the interstates and thruways, the Lehigh Valley of Northampton and Lehigh counties was a relatively remote place with quiet villages and small towns that were growing steadily into prosperous cities.

Those places were populated by immigrants from many nations who brought their cultures, traditions and superstitions into the hills and valleys washed by the Lehigh and Delaware rivers.

Tales of witchcraft, hexes, and strange customs were whispered throughout the land and kept alive through generations.

Most of those generations are themselves long gone. And, most of those traditions and superstitions were prevalent when the Lehigh Valley was largely populated by settlers from Germany.

These were the "Pennsylvania Germans," or as they were erroneously but popularly known, "Pennsylvania Dutch" (a corruption of "Deutsch," as in their home country, Deutschland).

Certainly, there are still large pockets of Pennsylvania Dutch in the Valley, but many of their more bizarre customs are lost in time and recorded only in the memories of the elders and the pages of books.

When the *Journal of American Folk-Lore* published accounts of some early beliefs in 1889, the traditions were already ebbing in acceptance and practice.

One tradition detailed was how Moravians in Bethlehem dealt with death. Noted culture and religion historian Israel Daniel Rupp wrote:

"The Corpse House, where on the death of a member of the society, the corpse is deposited for three days, is worthy of a notice.

"When a death occurs, a part of the choir ascend the church cupola or steeple, where a requiem or funeral hymn is played for the departed, and the melancholy notes as they fall on the ear in a calm morning are particularly solemn and impressive. The body on the third day is removed form the Corpse House, the mourners place themselves around it, and after several strains of solemn music, the procession forms a line of march to the grave, preceded by the band, still playing, which is continued some time after the coffin is deposited."

The Journal entry also noted that when someone died in a house, all mirrors were turned around to face the wall. "Otherwise," it noted, "the first person to see his image in any one of them will be sure to die within a year."

The eyes of the deceased were covered with copper pennies, and then with a piece of linen with embroidered edges. Upon burial, the coin and cloth were removed, but placed inside the the coffin before it was lowered into the grave.

Dead bodies supposedly had abilities to cure and correct the ills and ailments of the living.

A corn could be removed by rubbing a small piece of cotton over it and, while no one was looking, placing the cloth in a coffin before the dead person was buried. As soon as dirt was shoveled over the coffin in the grave, the corn would begin to disappear.

And, if the hand of a corpse was rubbed across a goiter, it, too, would gradually vanish.

Omens of death abounded in the old days. If an apple tree bloomed out of season on someone's property, someone in that family was sure to die in short order. And, a cricket chirping inside a house or horses running in the pasture were considered harbingers of death.

Beliefs in and fear of witchcraft and what the

"Dutch" called hexerei loomed over the superstitious society like low, dark clouds.

A story came out of the Trexlertown area regarding a family named Weiler who had for some reason angered a woman who lived on a nearby farm. That was not good, as the woman was regarded as a witch.

In retaliation for whatever the Weilers did, the woman placed a most unusual curse on them.

Whenever anyone came to call on the Weilers, their three daughters would suddenly turn into snakes!

They would slither across the floor and make their way to the upper ledge of the wainscoting before just as suddenly reverting back to their human forms.

The curse was apparently lifted after about three months. But, in that time, many visitors attested to the freaky phenomenon.

Family feuds and disagreements in everyday life back then were believed to carry on into the afterlife. Folklorist Walter James Hoffman wrote of one such incident in 1889.

A gruff and greedy chap known as "Old Kern" was feared in northern Northampton County for his evil ways. Some believed he was sent here by the devil himself, and when he died it was thought that he was called back to satan's lair.

There was a Mrs. Kern, and upon the death of

her husband she started hearing and seeing things that convinced her that his spirit remained in their house. Disembodied footsteps and knocking sounds, doors creaking open and closed, and other noises were attributed to the ghost of "Old Kern."

The widow asked neighbors and family members to stay with her, but not a one could endure the mysterious and disturbing clatter.

Eventually, the 19th century version of ghost hunters was called in to investigate. Several reliable young men stayed in the house for several days and nights and made an honest effort to find rational and natural explanations for the phenomena.

Try as they may have, they could not come up with any resolutions.

Mrs. Kern was so distressed by the prospect that her husband's ghost haunted the house that she soon abandoned it and moved far, far away.

VUE WITH A BOO!

Few would argue that the most "famous" ghost in Easton is Freddie, who haunts the State Theatre.

Freddie's meanderings were detailed in our first *Ghost Stories of the Lehigh Valley* book, and they seem to be limited to the stage and auditorium of the magnificent showplace.

But, if Freddie ever decided to wander out the front doors of the State Theatre, Phyllis O'Donnell would have a great view. That's exactly why she named her antique shop at 466 Northampton Street Phyl's Theatre Vue Antiques.

The building across from the theater was once an Army-Navy supply and surplus store, and that fact plays a major role in what Phyllis said is the story of a ghost that has seemingly come and gone from her shop.

"When I moved the antique shop in here," Phyllis said, "a man happened to come in and he told me he sensed a spirit here."

Phyllis admits to being sensitive, but as a healer, not as one who can detect apparitions. So, she was naturally intrigued by the possibility that she shared her antique shop space with a ghost.

"The man told me our ghost was an old Navy

guy, and he wants to be called 'Chief.'"

That, of course alludes to the enlisted rating of Chief Petty Officer in the Navy.

Phyllis said the customer told her the Chief inhabited the store, totally ignoring that it was no longer the kind of place he might have opted to shop in his Navy days.

She added that other people have come into the Theatre Vue with no knowledge of that original report and have also told her that they believed the spirit of an old sailor was within its walls.

"And then, back around 2006," she continued, "a man who was doing work on my front windows told me he happened to look over at one of the security camera monitors and saw what he described as a 'snowy' form coming straight up one of the aisles. He flipped out! He's a real tough guy, but that scared him and he went out of here like a bat out of hell!"

The building has had many tenants over the years, and was once the Boas Beer Salon and German Emigrant Boarding House. So, it could be haunted by any number of ghosts.

But, Phyllis was recently told the Chief was no longer showing up for the ethereal muster there. "I think he was here for a uniform or something that had to do with the Army-Navy store," she said.

And now that it's an antique store, perhaps he set sail for somewhere else.

SPIRITS OF THE
SAYRE MANSION

Robert Sayre wanted to live near where he worked. So, in 1858, he and his family moved into a house near his place of employment.

It was not a typical workplace. It was not a typical home. And, Robert Sayre was not a typical employee.

In fact, Sayre was the boss of the Lehigh Valley Railroad and son of William Sayre, who with Asa Packer helped develop the Lehigh Coal & Navigation Co. canal system. He parlayed his father's connections and his own skills into another transportation network that helped propel the Lehigh Valley–and America–full steam ahead into the Industrial Revolution.

As a teenager, Robert Heysham Sayre impressed his father and Packer with his engineering skills. But, the younger Sayre used those skills and intuition to build his own empire that would render his father's canals outmoded.

The timing of technology was perfect for Robert Sayre. In 1840, anthracite-fueled blast furnaces were being built, and iron was being produced in several communities throughout the valley.

Asa Packer saw the need for a coal carrier that would be faster and less dependent on the weather. He took Robert Sayre under his wing and financed construction of the railroad. At 27, Robert Sayre became its superintendent and chief engineer.

Blind in one eye, devoutly religious, and a voracious reader, Sayre ran a tight ship, er, railroad from its headquarters in Mauch Chunk (now Jim Thorpe) and Philadelphia. But, he was the classic "hands-on" manager and decided to move the company's offices, and his residence, to Bethlehem.

There, the Lehigh Valley met the North Penn railroad at a very busy junction. There, the Bethlehem Iron Works was prospering. There, Robert Sayre reckoned, is where the action was and where he wanted to be.

Bethlehem was a boom town. And shortly after he moved into his Fountain Hill mansion in 1858,

Sayre provided a few booms of his own. He was the benefactor of several cultural institutions and his corporate leadership vaulted the city into national prominence.

Robert Sayre died in 1907, and his family continued to occupy the Gothic Revival home until 1916. The building then went through several transformations in ensuing decades, including a term as a Lehigh University fraternity house and as an apartment building.

In 1993, it underwent extensive renovations and emerged as the stunning B&B that stands tall over the city.

Framed within two acres on Wyandotte Street, the Sayre Mansion Bed & Breakfast offers world-class accommodations–and a mystery or two.

Carrie Ohlandt is an innkeeper of what is called "the Lehigh Valley's premier urban inn." She told me it would appear that some of its previous residents so loved the place that they may never have left.

"I have never had a firsthand experience here," she said, "but the reports that we get are very interesting."

They are reports of ghostly forms and figures in at least two of the 18 guest rooms of the main house.

Imagine you glance into a mirror when a faint form begins to materialize just over your shoulder.

The mirror in Room 23 of the Sayre Mansion B&B. It is there that guests have reported seeing the image of a woman's face peering over their shoulder as they looked into the mirror.

You try to focus on the unnerving image, but it is at first just a blur. Then, it seems to take the shape of shoulders, a neck, and a head. Milliseconds pass, but you are riveted to the sight. Gradually, you discern the facial features of a woman. You squint, and then you squirm because what you are seeing simply should not be there.

Then, in a flash, the apparition vanishes!

That scenario has played out more than once in room 23, which was once the bed chamber of Mrs. Sayre, the mistress of the mansion.

"Usually," Carrie said, "the guests have reported seeing it in the middle of the night when they have awakened to use the bathroom or whatever. It's always the same mirror in that same room."

Although it has not been, and maybe never will be confirmed that it is the ghost of Mrs. Sayre, it is reasonable to speculate that her energy may remain in the mansion she so dearly loved.

Mrs. Sayre' nocturnal perambulations are not the only signs of spirit activity in the Sayre Mansion.

"We have another room where we have had two different reports of people sighting a presence," Carrie continued. "One person reported seeing something that came out of the wall and walk across the room. They said it was a dark shape."

That phenomenon has taken place in room 32,

which is on the third floor, where children and household staff once resided. Other guests have told the innkeepers that they felt there were strong, but benign energies on that third floor.

According to research, there were three family deaths in the main house, all of natural causes. It is said that during its frat house days, a young man hanged himself in the conservatory.

So, a solid baseline could be established with these passings. Thus, it could also be argued successfully that the Sayre Mansion is "enchanted" by the energies that linger there.

"Most of the time," Carrie said, "the guests who told us about their experiences here have been embarrassed to ask if we have any ghosts here."

That, of course, is a good sign that their encounters with the unknown were real and their reports, however scant in detail, were honest.

Carrie Ohlandt is unconcerned that the stories of ghostly goings-on there may make some guests uncomfortable.

"This is an historic house," she said. "Lots of fans of historic houses actually like for there to be a haunting in it. It gives it a certain charm and character."

In the nearly 40 years I have been investigating and writing about haunted places, I have come across hundreds of historic buildings that have had stories to be told.

My *Cape May Ghost Stories* trilogy serves as a model for discussing the impact of an alleged haunting on an historic building.

The charming Victorian city on the southern tip of New Jersey just, well, *looks* like it should be haunted. Its gingerbread homes and gaslit, tree-shaded streets seem to be veritable breeding grounds of ghostly activity.

The decision to have a closer look at the ghost stories in Cape May was a "no brainer." And, as it is known for its quaint B&Bs and inns, those places were the logical starting points.

As my efforts broadened, I discovered that many of those B&Bs were inhabited by ethereal entities.

But, an odd thing happened while on the way to Cape May ghost research.

Here is a graphic example using arbitrary figures.

If I went to 25 B&Bs and asked if they had any stories of hauntings, perhaps 15 said "yes."

Of those 15, however, perhaps eight said they did not want their ghost stories published in a book. *"It would be **bad for business**,"* they maintained.

The other seven had no problems with relating their experiences for any and all to read.

So, those B&Bs and their ghosts were included in *Cape May Ghost Stories, Book One.*

It wasn't too very long after the publication of what turned out to be a very successful book that two or three of those B&Bs that declined to release their stories called.

"How come you didn't use our story," they asked.

*"Because you said it would be **bad for business** and didn't want it used,"* I replied.

But what those businesses saw was that after the book reached the readers, many of those readers came to stay or dine in the establishments that allowed their stories to be told.

The ghost stories were, in the main, **good for business**.

There was, of course, a second Cape May Ghost Stories book, and some of those first-time holdouts relented and related their stories.

In an online bookseller's reader's review of one of my other books, the self-proclaimed reviewer noted, "It seems as if ghosts tend to haunt mostly businesses that stand to benefit from being labeled as haunted."

I wanted to at once mock and mourn that reader's assessment.

But here is the reality. Here is why any sensitive and sensible reader would understand quickly exactly why so many B&Bs, hotels, taverns, inns, and historic sites just seem to have ghost stories to tell and why they appear in ghost story books around the world.

First, the reader should have a deep appreciation for this reality.

It is to the eternal credit of the B&B, hotel, tavern, inn, and historical site owners that they have lovingly, faithfully, and often expensively restored, refurbished, and reopened their properties as public places.

Throughout the Lehigh Valley are many such places that have been maintained or rescued and used for commercial purposes.

And, in many of those structures, the ghosts came along for the restoration ride.

It is in those places that the reader of this kind of book can enjoy a meal in a haunted dining room or (try to) sleep in a haunted guest room or look over their shoulders for a ghost that may appear in a mirror or wander from a wall.

And, if the owners or operators make a few bucks out of it, well, so be it. They pay nothing to be in the book, and we pay nothing for their stories.

I have watched as bits of history, and often *haunted* history, are destroyed and demolished. It sickens me.

I use my native county, Berks, as a prime example. Just as throughout Lehigh and Northampton counties, Berks has been victimized by rampant development and growth in recent years.

Too often left in the wake of that have been historic or locally significant places that have been razed for a convenience store, mall, fast-food joint, or gas station. Maps of Berks, Lehigh, and Northampton counties are dotted and scarred by this kind of "progress."

So, to the innkeeper, restaurateur, or raconteur who spends money, time, and love to save a 200-year old hotel from the wrecker's ball or spare a 150-year old mansion and convert it to a B&B...thank you!

Thank you on behalf of this writer, those readers who just might drop by, and thanks mostly on behalf of the spirits for whom you have provided a comfortable habitat.

THOSE ON "THE OTHER SIDE" OF "THE OTHER SIDE"

Any self-respecting ghost hunter would leap at the opportunity to investigate a haunting at a restaurant called "The Other Side."

The name conjures up the euphemism for what lies beyond our existence on this mortal coil.

At the Neffs Hotel in the village of Neffs in North Whitehall Township, it is simply the name of the room on "the other side" of the wall.

"Hmm," mused Kelly Schaffer, "I never even thought of that other meaning!"

And, is it turns out for this ghost-hunting writer, there are those on "the other side" in "The Other Side."

Kelly, who with her husband Zane own the ca. 1850 hotel, has grown to accept the ghosts there. She speaks of them calmly and casually, as they have become a part of everyday life in The Other Side.

"When my husband used to sleep upstairs," she said, "he saw some things. So, yes, we believe we have a ghost or two here."

Indeed, before the building was remodeled, Zane slept in one of the old hotel rooms upstairs.

143

On one occasion, he woke up in the middle of the night to see a mysterious yellow-green glow coming through the transom above the door and the sliver of space between the bottom of the door and the floor. He was stone-cold sober and not dreaming. When he mentioned it to one of the old-timers who had frequented the place for many years, they told him it was "just" the ghost of Neffs–as if it was to be totally expected.

Kelly said the most unexpected, and thus most intriguing reports have come out of the blue from customers.

"One man was sitting at a table and he called the waitress over and asked if an older lady once owned the place. She said, yes, figuring he was referring to my mother-in-law, who owned it before us.

"Then, he told her that he had seen someone standing in the doorway. He described it as the ghost of what he called a 'cranky, older lady,' just standing there, watching at the main restaurant area.

"He said the woman he saw was staring out into the restaurant, and was not happy," Kelly laughed as she then realized he was not referring to her mother-in-law.

"He said she was dressed in old-fashioned clothing, probably from back in the horse-and-buggy era."

Kelly said she was in the restaurant with one customer just before closing time one night when she heard coughing and footsteps from an area of the building she knew was unoccupied.

She also recalled reports from two waitresses, who each saw, at the very same time, a figure pass through the main restaurant.

"It wasn't a clear image, they told me. They could see right through it. They were working at the salad bar and both turned to the left at the same time and saw it move from one side of the room to the other," she said.

"We hear footsteps a lot," she continued. "Before it was remodeled, the upstairs was just one, big storage room with hardwood floors. Many, many times, we would hear the clear sound of footsteps walking across the upstairs floor. Now that there are apartments up there and they are carpeted, we no longer hear that."

Both patrons and staff members have also detected the strong presence of a male spirit in the old hotel.

Zane's mother, Louise Frederick, grew up in nearby Ormrod and knew the hotel as a customer and, for ten years before she purchased the hotel in 1992, as an employee.

She had many of her own unexplainable experiences there, and believed the energies that toyed with her senses were those of a previous owner, Alton Kern. She and others would attribute any and all strange happenings to Alton. She felt that his was a beneficent spirit, and was pleased at the sweeping improvements she made when she took over operations.

Louise collected reports of ghostly encounters from employees, customers, and family members on every floor of the building.

The "cranky old woman" seems to be the dominant spirit there now, as some believe Alton has crossed over to the other side–the "other" other side.

The ghostly activity seems confined these days to the restaurant and bar areas. And, whomever or whatever the residual spirits may be, they have just become characters in the comfortable country tavern.

"Oh, there's definitely a presence here. It really doesn't bother us, though," Kelly said, with qualifications. "Well, there are times when somebody's here alone, and it's a little bit scarier. But nobody has ever experienced anything that's frightening. You just see forms and figures, just walking around.

"There are times that items are moved around, and things disappear and reappear in strange places. That can be frustrating. But, other than that, they don't bother anybody. They're just kind of around."

THE SPIRIT OF THE KNAUSS HOMESTEAD: IS IT ELIZABETH... ...OR ELIZABETH?

Emmaus is among the most charming and historic towns in the Lehigh Valley. Its proud past prosperous present commingle in a busy downtown that personifies the sometimes elusive image of small town America.

At the heart of the history of Emmaus are the Moravians who established an enclave there in 1759. And, among the names of the most prominent citizens of 18th century Emmaus is Knauss.

It was Sebastian Knauss who donated land for the establishment of that original Moravian congregational village.

His legacy is preserved at the home built by his son, Heinrich, in 1777. At the rear of 164 Main Street, the Knauss Homestead stands as a borough-owned, privately-maintained house museum.

As this is not a history book, but a ghost book, my first question to the keepers of the Knauss

Homestead was if any spirits roam within its walls.

Linda Burkhardt, of the Knauss Homestead Preservation Society, answered my question with a resounding "hmm, it could be!"

Not entirely willing to commit herself to saying the building is, in the vernacular, *haunted*, she did recall an incident that left even the most staunch skeptic wondering if the ghost of a young woman is a permanent resident in the Knauss house.

Linda recalled a 1995 open house of the homestead when a group of girl scouts was in attendance.

As the event was wrapping up, several of the scouts must have been taken back a bit by the sight of a winsome young woman's candlelit face staring down at them from a second floor window at the rear of the building.

Historical sites often have costumed reenactors portray characters from the past. But that night, at that place, there was no young female reenactor in that second story window. There were no candles there.

"The Girl Scouts were waiting for their parents outside the back of the house facing the parking lot," Linda said. "They ran in and encouraged the one girl who knew me personally to ask if they could go upstairs. When I responded 'no, it is not open to public, it's unsafe,' she told me what they saw."

That night, at that place, those girl scouts could very well have seen a ghost.

So many visitors saw the same figure in the same window that the preservationists gave the apparition a name—Elizabeth.

The name is in remembrance of one known death of a young girl there, a girl named Elizabeth Knauss, who died in the house on February 4, 1780. She was the daughter of Heinrich and Anna Maria Knauss.

While it could really be Elizabeth's spirit that has remained there for more than 229 years, some things just don't quite match up.

According to research, Elizabeth was just about five and a half years old when she passed away. The figure seen in the window was described as a girl in her early teens.

Again not ready to dismiss the notion of a ghost in the homestead, Linda Burkhardt theorized that the lonely little lady in the upstairs window might instead be another Elizabeth.

"According to the girls' description of an older girl," Linda said, "I searched my records and came upon Elizabeth Giering, who was born on December 6, 1757. Since it happened to be December 6, 1995, when the open house was held, I attributed the sighting to her."

After the girl scouts left that night in 1995,

Linda and another member of the preservation society board decided to have a look around the second floor, with the remote chance that they might encounter Elizabeth...or Elizabeth.

Linda said she did hear some thumps and bumps as they ascended the staircase. But, when they carefully checked the upstairs rooms for any sight of a spook, they found nothing more frightening than a dead mouse.

That's right, a mouse in the house of Knauss.

The (not haunted) Emmaus Moravian Church.

150

EVPs IN THE INN

The village of Hereford has somewhat of an identity crisis.

It is in Hereford Township, Berks County. But, throw a stone one direction and it'll land in Montgomery County. Throw one another direction and it'll land in Lehigh County. OK, it would take Herculean stone throws, but you get the picture.

In fact, township children attend a school district based in Montgomery County. Township residents have phone numbers with a 215 prefix, and Hereford is 34 miles from the Berks County seat of Reading but only 13 miles from the Lehigh County courthouse in Allentown.

All that geopolitical information aside, let us now explore an early 18th century inn where several ghosts dwell, and where members of the Lehigh Anomalous Phenomenon Investigation Society (LAPIS) have spent many hours searching for them.

The investigators were invited to try to confirm what almost everyone who works at Poor

Richard's Historic Hereford Inn already knew–that it was haunted.

Tina Mack, daughter-in-law of owners Carol and Richard Mack, was already convinced.

"I saw a ghost in the basement," she said. "I felt a presence around me, and I looked up to see a man standing right in front of me. He was heavyset, and was wearing a long coat and a top hat."

A bit shaken, Tina hastened upstairs and told her mother-in-law about her experience. When Tina described the apparition, Carol calmly said it fit the description of August Spaar, who owned the inn for many years. Carol then showed Tina a picture of Mr. Spaar, and it closely resembled the image she saw in the basement.

Augustus D. Spaar was the hotel's popular proprietor from 1912 to the early 1950s.

Built as the Sand Springs Hotel in 1830, the Hereford Inn has been an eating and drinking establishment and boarding house ever since its opening. Its present owners maintain an extensive collection of photographs, documents, and artifacts related to its history, and have no problem with the prospect that the building is haunted.

Since seeing "Augustus" in the basement, she has had several other encounters.

"My husband's sister and I heard a woman screaming at the top of the steps that lead into the basement," she said. "I was bartending and she was bringing beer up from downstairs. So, she thought it was me screaming and I thought it was her screaming. When we met at the top of the steps, we both realized that neither one of us had screamed. There was no other woman in the building at the time."

Other employees, family members, and customers have witnessed shadowy forms, watched as beer taps turned on and off on their own, and listened as disembodied footsteps, knocking sounds, and muffled conversation were heard.

Tina said they have plunged headfirst into attempting to pick up Electronic Voice Phenomena (EVP) with the help of the Lehigh Anomalous Phenomenon Investigation Society (LAPIS).

Mary Ann Tettemer of LAPIS conducted a recent investigation there. "We caught a few EVPs," she said, "one of which was a name– 'Trumble' or maybe 'Trumbauer,' but I could not connect it with anyone."

During other recording sessions, Tina said several other EVPs were captured. "One was '4-4-5.' We had no idea what that might have meant, but it came across real clearly. And, we picked up many other EVPs we couldn't explain. We have heard, or interpreted, EVPs that seem to say 'Please stand back,' 'Please leave me alone,' and 'Mary, help me!'"

One LAPIS investigator even asked questions in German, which would have been the native language of many local residents (including any named Trumbauer) over the centuries. The group received EVP replies, but they were indistinguishable.

The epicenter of much electronic phenomena in the Hereford Inn is Room Three, one of the upstairs chambers that comprise the inn's boarding house.

In it, the distinct and disturbing sound of heavy breathing or sighing has been recorded, as well as the knocking on the door (when no one was present to knock), and the clicking of old-style door latches, which are not on the doors there.

LAPIS investigators have also set up video cameras in an attempt to catch visual apparitions, but have had limited success with that.

"That Room Three definitely has a lot of activity," said Mary Ann Tettemer. We also had a lot of Electromagnetic Field (EMF) spikes and crashes that correlate with the EVPs. One night alone, we had more than 30 EVPs."

Tina said there is nothing threatening about the ghosts that she is certain walk among the living at the Hereford Inn. They are, she believes, just part and parcel to life–and death–and afterlife–in an old country inn.

154

GHOSTS FROM
HERE AND THERE, THEN AND NOW

An inevitable and anticipated postscript to the publication of a book such as this is the flurry of letters (then) and emails (now) that arrive after the book hits the bookstores.

The original *Ghost Stories of the Lehigh Valley* was released in 1993 and has not been out of print since then.

I have written 14 books between that book and this, and in the years between what is now Book One was published and the commencement of research for this book, I have accumulated a thick file folder of stories related by readers. In this chapter, I present some of those stories, guarding the privacy of some of the respondents by not using their real names.

The first is the account from a young woman who was a student at Cedar Crest College when she read the short passage about a ghost named Wanda who, according at least to rumor, haunted the Butz Hall dormitory.

Mailed shortly after the first book was released, the letter detailed the writer's experience in a room I'll identify only as being in, as she described it, "Butz Second West."

It was in that dorm where "Wanda" supposedly killed herself–although college officials staunchly denied that any student, in any dorm up to that time, had ever committed suicide there.

"I worked as an Orientation Staff two weeks prior to classes," she wrote. "There was nobody else living on my side of the hall except for me during that period of time.

"During the first days living there I started decorating my room and listened to music. I went to the book store to buy my books and I saw the book on ghost stories in the Lehigh Valley. I began to read it that same day.

"I read the introduction and a paragraph that said that when you turn on a radio or television, 'images will emerge from the atmosphere.'"

The passage in the introduction explained how invisible signals are sent to electronic devices and are turned into sounds and sights when those devices are switched on. The thought at once freaked her out and confused her.

"I slept that night with my alarm clock radio on, thinking that they will leave my room (the atmosphere). But, I understood wrong. It meant that they will *enter* the atmosphere!"

Although the radio was playing, she managed to fall asleep. Actually, she awoke in the middle of the night to the silence caused when a wall hanging fell, smothered the radio, and muffled the sound.

"There was no way that the poster could have fallen by itself onto the radio," she said. "If it just dropped from the wall, it would have landed on the dresser."

The coed was miffed and a bit frightened by the incident. She was certain that "Wanda" was the culprit.

"When my roommate moved in, I told her about what happened to me and I told her that 'Wanda' was a good spirit and she had nothing to fear.

"But, I told her, be aware. Anything could happen."

And, things did happen. Eventually, the student called her grandmother, whom she described as a medium and spiritual advisor.

"She told me to put a glass of water with sugar in it and 'Wanda' would leave us alone. And, she did–for a while. But soon, other things started to happen. Things fell from my bulletin board and my walls, and things would disappear from my room. My roommate's and my alarm clocks would go off without either she or I setting them. I would also feel cold pockets in the hall and sometimes felt the presence of entities around me."

As she had just read the story about Wanda, perhaps it was the power of suggestion that led to the young student attributing the anomalies to her ghost. Or, perhaps it really was Wanda's way to welcome her to college life.

•

Leonard Shupp of Whitehall provided the tale of an apparition at an old farmhouse in Ballietsville, Lehigh County.

"It all began about 1929-32," he wrote, while the Ormrod plant of the Lehigh Portland Cement Co. was still in full swing, around the clock.

"A report circulated among the local citizens that there was a 'ghost' or 'spook' to be seen at the old Mickley Farmhouse in Ballietsville.

"At dark, people from all walks of life, all ages, would gather at the side of the Mickley house–their automobile lights directed toward a second story window.

"When the shift changed at LPC, many men would come to see the apparition. I was about seven to ten years old when one night I went with my dad to see the ghost. Hundreds of people gathered under the window, on the lawn, while others remained in their automobiles, motors running and lights on.

"Someone would yell 'there it is!' and all eyes would be directed upon the windows.

"My dad and I never saw anything. Yet, others claimed they saw the ghost cross over in front of the window. This went on for years until the Mickley house was torn down or burned down–I don't remember.

"There was an old rumor rampant, that either a family member or a hired person mysteriously disappeared one time, and the body was allegedly buried in the basement. But, the spirit of the person still haunted the house."

The old homestead was also the site of an Indian attack in 1763, and the energies of several family members killed then may also have been imprinted there.

•

An Orefield woman sent a sad story about her brief but powerful encounter with a spirit she said she could easily identify.

"My husband shot himself in March, 1980," she said. "A year or so after that, I was in bed and turned on my side. All of a sudden, I felt someone getting into bed with me.

"I got really scared. And then, I felt an arm go over my waist. Then, I heard a man say, very softly, the Lord's Prayer."

As frightening as the experience must have been, the woman said she was somehow contented and managed to fall asleep.

She told several friends and relatives about her experience, and most marveled that she could go to sleep after it. One neighbor said it may just have been the "right time" for her husband to say good bye to her.

She added that nothing like it ever happened again, and that yes, it was in that very bedroom where her husband shot himself.

•

Another story of a lost love came from a Lehigh County woman who said she was glad to read that things that happened to her and her daughter had happened to other people. She noted that until she was impacted by the inexplicable, she was not a believer. Now, she is.

The woman's husband died in the Lehigh

Valley Hospital after being burned over 90 percent of his body in a fire. "He lasted four weeks until they pulled the life machine cord," she said. "After that, strange things happened."

She said her husband spent much time in the basement of their home, tinkering on various projects.

Shortly after his death, lights in the basement began to turn themselves on and off. Neighbors first noticed the lights going on while no one was home.

The woman also believes her husband may have saved her and their daughter's life when he "signaled" them from the basement that carbon monoxide was building up as the furnace was malfunctioning and prompted them to call a repairman.

And, another signal coming from beyond might have come on a grim, rainy day.

"My girlfriend took me to the cemetery where my husband is buried," she said. "I heard spooky organ music, so I didn't stay there long. I looked all over and nobody was around. I asked my friend if she had heard it and she said she didn't hear a thing. When I got back to her car, the organ music stopped."

•

A reader sent a clipping from the *Morning Call* in which the gifted and prolific newspaperman

Frank Whelan recounted a bizarre case of suspected witchcraft in Allentown in 1911.

It involved a mysterious, exotic woman named Meta Immerman who had come to Allentown from the Upper West Side of Manhattan, where she ran a prestigious dressmaking shop.

Neighbors in the 200 block of S. 13th Street were suspicious of the attractive woman from the moment she moved into a third floor room in an apartment building owned by George Kipp, a butcher.

The Kipps lived on the first floor and Mr. and Mrs. John Sober lived on the second.

Mrs. Sober and Mrs. Kipp quickly built up a fascinating but flawed case against Ms. Immerman, questioning her eccentric lifestyle.

They caught her eating raw eggs and chestnuts as meals. They spied her walking barefoot in the yard and through a nearby park.

It's not clear whether they confronted the woman or she volunteered the information, but Meta told the busybodies that she loved nature and natural foods, and it was all part of her health regimen.

One day, John Sober took ill and was advised by his wife to visit a powwow doctor named Kistler. The "doctor" diagnosed Sober as being "bewitched."

Stunned by the revelation, Sober told his wife

what Dr. Kistler had said. She knew right away who had placed a "hex" on him. It had to be Meta Immerman. The raw eggs? The chestnuts? The walking barefoot? All hallmarks of a *witch!*

The Sobers and Kipps reviewed their contacts with the stranger from New York. John Sober remembered the time he helped her lug her suitcase up the stairs. That was when he "hoodooed" him, he reckoned!

Yes, he believed she cast an evil spell over him.

The Kipps and Sobers agreed that the matter called for intervention by the authorities.

Apparently, the Allentown police department of 1911 was as enlightened as those it served. Officers arrived at the Kipp house and, while shouting, "Come down, witch!" went upstairs to take the suspected sorceress into custody.

A crowd had gathered, and some called for a stoning of the "witch." Some young boys actually did throw stones at her.

The matter reached a city alderman's court, and it was a classic "he said/she said" case. Kipp claimed Immerman was a witch, and Immerman denied any such notion. But, as Kipp was local and Immerman was a transplant, the alderman sentenced the woman to 48 hours in the lockup.

Incensed, Ms. Immerman threatened to sue the Kipps upon her release from jail. But, a lawyer she consulted said that she would likely never win the suit.

Meta Immerman returned to Manhattan and was never heard from again in Allentown. But, the case drew the attention of Dr. John Kloss, who operated the Peaceful Valley Retreat in Fountain Hill. It was he who invited Ms. Immerman to the area, hoping she would help him establish a natural health hospital in the hills south of Bethlehem.

He had actually visited Meta in her room in Allentown, and had his own questions about the integrity of her landlord and neighbors. "Ms. Immerman was too bright, intelligent, and up to date for the people in the neighborhood," he said.

He also recalled an incident when the woman was chased down the street when she performed one of her acts of "witchcraft" with what the unenlightened residents were sure was a "magic wand." After all, in Allentown in 1911, few people had ever come across anyone who, with the flick of one finger, could cast a beam of light across a room.

These days, we call that "magic wand" a flashlight.

•

Other readers spoke of the ghost of a gypsy king who rises and glides through Ontelaunee Park in New Tripoli; a wandering Revolutionary War-era spirit who maintains an eternal vigil in the

Union and West End Cemetery in Allentown; a ghost in the post office in Bangor; an apparition that has been spotted desceding a stone staircase along the Monocacy Creek in Bethlehem, and a specter that frequents the shelter near Bake Oven Knob.

With the publication of this second volume of Lehigh Valley tales, a fresh crop of emails is sure to sprout.

I look forward to reaping the harvest.